Cancer Was My Blessing!

By Yolanda Commack

Introduction

I am Yolanda Commack; aka Lonnie to my friends and family. There are several labels that could be placed on me; auto worker, fitness trainer, single parent, and one-year survivor of triple negative breast cancer. Reality is I could be any woman; your aunt, your sister, your friend. I wanted to write this book because too many times people think that traumatic life events signal the end of the road. Well, I'm here to say, "No, it's not!" Life is what you make it. When stricken with the drama that life can bring, you have to ask yourself, "Am I going to sit back and dwell on my circumstances, or am I going come up with a plan to work through them and become victorious?" When I asked myself that very question the answer was easy. I had to fight. There was no way I was going down with anything less than that!

From the moment I received my diagnosis of breast cancer, I told myself that no matter how hard or tough things got, I would stay positive and keep a smile on my face; even if that meant smiling with tears rolling down my face. The way I look at it, we can't control the hand that we are dealt in life; all we can control is our reaction to it. And I was determined that my reaction would be as positive as possible.

I'm a firm believer that sometimes the Lord will allow things to happen to us in life in order to get our attention. As I heard the knocking of God on my door of life, I had to open it and be ready for what He had waiting for me on the other side. If I was going to have faith in Him during the good times, that meant I had to have that same amount of faith during the bad. What better way for Him to get my attention than to touch my health—the very thing that I lived and strived for. My health and fitness—the very way I defined myself to the rest of the world. And yet He did it all while I was on a platform for everyone to see me going through my pain and my treatments. Pursuing the career that I loved meant that there was no way I could hide what I was going through as cancer began to attack me. But I had to fight. No matter how many would see my personal battle on center stage. I had to fight. I was determined to be strong inside and out; and that is exactly what I did. Health and fitness are my world, so there was no way I could go hide under a rock just because my body was being attacked. I had to deal with the hand I was dealt and do it in a manner that was still inspirational to those who were looking up to me.

So I did it. I cried on the inside and still enjoyed life on the outside. Losing hair and teeth all while still loving what I do. Cancer would not define me. I still trained the people that had come to depend on me for improving their fitness. I just learned how to train my body on the outside to continue to move on every day as if things were normal; all the while, I had to emotionally strengthen myself to tie my hair up and control my emotions on the inside. People were counting on me for physical training and guidance. There was no way I was going to allow the fact that I was dealing with my own mortality to be a roadblock in doing what I was put here on Earth to do. So I stayed the course. I dealt with the cancer all while continuing to train my clients. I wanted them to know, "If I can work out with what I'm going through, than you certainly have no excuse for not doing the same."

I'm still dealing with the hand I have been dealt. God never promised that life would be easy...only that it would be worth it. Currently, I'm losing my son to behavioral issues, and taking care of my mother after a stroke. Both of which can sometimes be heavy on the shoulders of this single mom. But let me tell you, there is a blessing in the lesson, because *CANCER WASN'T MY CURSE; IT WAS MY BLESSING!*

The Day My Sister Shaved Her Head

DEDICATIONS

This book is first dedicated to my heavenly Father who has brought me through the storm, even when, at times, I wanted to be left right in the middle of the storm that I was in.

Special thanks to my parents for loving and encouraging me through everything I set my mind out to do. Their support was the wind beneath my wings allowing me to fly. To my sisters and brothers, who may not always show they are proud of me, but I see it in their eyes every time they look at me and I feel it in my heart. To my children, Trinity and Koreyon, who shared me with my job, my training, and the world; everything I do is for the two of you.

I would also like to thank my pastors; past and present. Brother Johnny and Pastor Newton, you have encouraged me in ways you would not believe. Rachell and Aisha, I can never fully express my appreciation for both of you doing everything I even hinted that I needed done. I even have a special appreciation and thanks for the friends and mates that turned their backs to me and talked about me; for even though you did not know it, your actions encouraged and strengthen me as well.

Heartfelt thanks to the nurses and doctors at the Cancer Center, who accepted me for Lonnie, and never told me to sit down and be quiet. To my friends at work, especially the two crybabies; Kerrie and Buffy, and to Jeremy and Carla and Grandma, thanks for your support. My friends Lesa, Rhonda, Bobo, Sean, Dada, Roger, Pat, Gina...you guys refused to feel sorry for me, and would not allow me to feel sorry for myself. I thank you for that!

To all my clients who I continually fuss at, the ones that I knew loved me even though they often acted as though I got on their nerves; Kim Littlejohn, Kim Jones, Janell, Nika, Tonya (BKA) LC, Sherri, Jamie, Dana, Lori and everyone else. I love you all, and it's too many of you to name. I'd also like to give a special shout out to Rhonda, Roz, my cousin April, and Tammy who all fought this cancer fight; we rock ladies!

I can't forget about sexy Shawna, Stacey Cole and Stacie Bobo. Beautiful Brenda, and Yolanda, *WE ARE ALL SURVIVORS!* My cry baby cousin Kim. Marsha you were a God send; I LOVE YOU GIRL! I can't leave out Trice and my barber Awri. My friend Yankee, who supported everything I have done; thanks to you and your beautiful wife.

To anyone I may have missed, please blame it to my head and not my heart; I thank you too from the bottom of heart!

The Loves Of My Life; Koreyon And Trinity

The Diagnosis!

I can't actually say why I checked under my right arm that day while I took a shower at my mom's house on a night in which I had stayed over to take care of her. Maybe my actions were prompted because I was close to forty years old and knew that I should be more concerned about my breasts; or maybe the inner voice speaking clearly in my ear knew something was wrong and told me to check it out for myself. I don't know what prompted my actions, but they were almost mechanical as if guided by something or someone other than myself. I remember the moment as if it were yesterday.

While in the shower, I lift my right arm and check around in a circular motion. *Humm, nothing*, I think to myself. So I feel around my breast, *humm, is that what I think it is?* My mind wanders as my fingertips caress a very small lump that kinda moves around when I touch it. *No big deal.* I say out loud to myself. *It's probably nothing, but I guess I will make an appointment to get it checked since it's time for a mammogram anyway.* It's November; I don't turn forty until July, so I tell myself that maybe I will just wait until then to get it checked out. I go ahead with my everyday routine. I'm not concerned; breast cancer doesn't run in my family. I eat right, I exercise at least six days a week, and I don't smoke and only socially drink. By all measures in my mind there's no need for me to worry about anything health wise.

Since Friday is my day off, I decide to make an appointment to have it checked out on the following Friday. After calling my doctor and making the appointment, the rest of my week is uneventful. When Friday approaches, I walk in the office of my primary doctor with no fear since in my mind I have nothing to worry about. The exam is routine in nature; nothing out of the ordinary, just the added procedure of checking of my breasts along with the usual checking of my vital signs. His hands are cold and I try not to make an already uncomfortable situation more awkward than it already is. It's best to not engage in small talk while someone is massaging your breasts.

His hands move in circular motions along my breasts and under my arms. Instantly I can tell that he feels the same lump that I did a week earlier. As his fingertips linger on the lump he says, "It's probably nothing to worry about, but let's just cut the lump out and do a biopsy on it just to be sure." I watch as my doctor scribbles notes in my medical file. He isn't concerned; so neither am I.

With his instructions still fresh on my mind, I leave his office and make an appointment to have the biopsy done on the following Friday so I won't have to take off work. My approach to the whole situation is a feeling of being numb; it all seems like nothing more than an inconvenience to me. I only agree to have the surgery because my doctor suggested I have it done. There's no need in avoiding it, I might as well get it over with so that I can get on with my life.

Friday approaches pretty quickly and I go in for the outpatient surgery that is supposed to dismiss any doubt that I am anything but okay. Just as the doctor had assured me, it was pretty quick and easy and I leave with only a couple of stitches as battle scars. As I leave his office, the doctor orders, "No lifting" and I go on with my day as normal. Being the hard-headed person that I am, I did my fitness class the next morning, lifting weights and training clients for an hour as if I had not even heard the doctor's words. I returned to work at *Ford* on Monday morning and continued my job of building trucks as I did every other day of the work week. In order to prove to my coworkers that I really had the surgery done, I showed them the stitches!

"What are you doing here?" they would all ask me with a look of disbelief that I was going about my day as if nothing had happened.

I would look them in the eye, laugh and say, "It's just a little sore, but not enough to make me take off work, or stop me from doing my fitness classes and take care of my mom three nights a week. Life goes on."

Before I know it, it's Friday, time to get my stitches out and get results from my doctor. I figure the appointment will be no big deal, so I tell my sisters and friends, "No, no...you guys don't have to go with me, I will be fine."

So with the reassurance I give to them and the confidence in my own words, I head to the doctor's office with just my boyfriend, at the time by my side. After the usual check in, the nurse calls my name. I walk into the small examining room and immediately I begin to joke with my doctor because he dresses so nice and always smells so good. His demeanor is strange because he is not laughing and joking with me as he normally does.

"Honey, I have some good news and bad news, which one do you want first?" His bedside manner is like it usually is, but it is wrapped with a serious tone that I am not used to him having.

As I look in his eyes, I'm thinking, *Ok, the bad news is that the darn stitches aren't healing like they should and can't come out yet*. So I say, "Give me the good news first 'Doctor Smell Good'."

"Ok, the stitches are ready to come out!" He says matter of factly.

"Ok, I'm confused now. So what's the bad news then?

He looks down, avoiding eye contact with me and says, "You have breast cancer."

Disbelief is my first reaction. I look at him and say, "Excuse me!"

"I'm sorry." he says, "but you have breast cancer."
The chair behind me cannot catch me fast enough. I sit down and say nothing. I couldn't have heard him right.

Me?

Cancer?

Lonnie?

How can that be? I can't get my mind to comprehend the words that have come out of his mouth.

As I try to digest what I have just been told, it seems as if the world is standing still. What felt like forever, turned out to be only about two minutes. I hold my head down and cry.

When the tears allow me to speak I say, "What do I need to do?"

He says, "Let's remove the lymph nodes under your arm and some from your breast to see if the cancer has spread. Then we will know the best treatment for you."
The ride home is a long one. I try to process the news as best I can. I lay my head down in my lap and cry. My boyfriend, at the time, rubs my back and says, "You're going to be ok." But his words don't have the conviction behind them to convince either of us.

We can't make it home soon enough for my liking and I walk in my house only to find my son is waiting on me for the news. I walk pass him and up to my room without saying a word. From behind me I can hear him say, "Is it bad news?"

My boyfriend responds for me. "Yes!"

I don't elaborate. I can't. I refuse to make him worry.

I refuse to cry in front of him. Instead I grab the car keys and leave the house. The car moves on autopilot. Before I know it, I am at my sister's house. She's not home. My car seeks refuge at my Dad's house. He's not there either. I continue to drive, crying uncontrollably saying, "Lord, what am I supposed to do?"

I am crying so hard I can't see. *Pull yourself together! You're going to be fine! Go home...your son is worried!* I chastise myself and head for home.

I walk in the house and assure my son that I'm going to be fine. Then I make my next appointment for the next Friday which was becoming a routine habit for me. Instinctively, I go ahead with my normal activities, working at *Ford*, conducting my fitness classes, taking care of my mom three nights a week, and taking care of my kids. Life has not skipped a beat despite the news I have been given. I won't allow it to change.

Before I know it, all of my family and coworkers know I have cancer. I see the fear and disbelief in their eyes as they look at me. My coworkers, who feel comfortable enough with me to ask the question, finally do.

"Why are you here Yolanda? Why are you working?" The question is asked more times than I care to hear it.

I smile and give the same response, "The same reason you are."

The week passes slowly and finally Friday comes and again, I undergo surgery. The waiting room is full of people who have come with me to show their support; my sisters, my brother-in-law and my friend Amanda, who brings a big plant. *Who the hell does she think is going to want to carry that home?* I think with a smile before the surgery begins. As I drift off to sleep under the anesthesia, I can feel the love

16

that surrounds me and I am thankful for it. My life and my prognosis are in the hands of the doctor and God.

I awake from the surgery with no complications and me, my sister Tonia, and Amanda go out to eat trying to have some resemblance of normalcy. Halfway through the dinner the pain medicine wears off and I can no longer stand the pain. With a forced smile I state, "Ok, I'm ready to go."

We cut the evening short and I go home, take my pain medication and drift off to Lala land. I lay awake in the middle of the night and raise my arm. It's a little sore, but I'm doing my classes in the morning at 9:00 a.m. come rain or shine! I'm sore, but determined to make it through my one-hour class and announce to anyone who looks at me with sympathy in their eyes that I will punch them in the stomach! And that is exactly what I do.

As I lay in bed on Saturday night, I'm sore and tired. Feelings of defeat invade my space. I say, "Lord, I know there's a lesson I'm supposed to learn from this; what is it?" His answer does not come. I resolve to be patient.

Sunday morning comes and I attend church as usual. Before I know it, I find myself standing before the congregation. I tell the church about the fight ahead of me and ask for prayer. I know I need help and prayer warriors and the unconditional strength of their prayers gives me peace.

Before I know it, it's Sunday night and true to form, I have done my class as scheduled. My underarm hurts and my stitches are red and swollen. But I don't have time to think about it or let it get me down. I have responsibilities to tend to; I can have a pity party later. I don't have time to allow the throbbing pain to get the best of me so I go stay at my mom's house as I was scheduled to do. Her stroke a year ago has left her unable to walk, so someone has to take care of her twenty-four hours a day. She's aware of my condition, so she doesn't want me to lift her. But it's my shift and no one else is there. I manage to give her the usual care that she needs in spite of my own pain.

For another week, life goes on as it did before the surgery. Everything has changed; yet everything has remained the same. Things are harder at home. I'm still cooking, cleaning and washing. I guess my family thinks, *Lonnie's strong, she can handle it.* I press on and do all what has to be done.
Finally Friday comes and my friend Lesa and sister Greta go with me to get my stitches out.

OUCH! It hurts so freaking bad! I'm not a punk girl or anything close to it; but man...it feels like he's ripping my underarm apart!

"I don't see any cancer in your lymph nodes; that's good! So all you are going to have to do is radiation."

"Ok, good. "So no chemo?" I ask.

"No." He says.

"Great! So I won't lose my hair?"

"No. Just eight weeks of radiation every day. It takes about fifteen minutes. You can even continue to work if you feel up to it."

Great! I think to myself as his words offer a bit of reassurance. I can battle cancer fifteen minutes a day for eight weeks, and still work and do my classes like I normally do. For the first time in two weeks, I exhale a bit.

"I'm going to send your chart over to the *Kansas City Cancer Center*, and after they look it over, they will call you to set up an appointment and let you know your treatment options."

Ok. Cool. I can handle that.

I was ready to fight and get it over with.

At least that's what I thought.

But just as soon as I was excited about not having to go through chemo, a wrench was dropped in my plans.

Q: WHAT HAS SHOCKED OR DEVASTATED YOU?

My Favorite Wig Mary J Blige

What? A Change In Plans?

A specialist at the Cancer Center called, they had reviewed my chart and I need to come in ASAP! That's all they would say over the phone.

UGH! OK. What about Friday because I'm not taking off work!

Ok was the response. Next Friday it is.
This time me and my best friend, who is my sister Tonia, head to the Cancer Center together to hear what the big deal is that can't wait until after the holiday. *Duh, it's almost Christmas, I have shopping to do.* We laugh and make jokes as we walk into the Cancer Center. Never in a million years had the thought that the news that I was about to receive would be something that was going to change my life forever. It never crossed any of our minds. Shoot, we had plans to meet my friends Sean and Bobo for a big party and concert night, that's just how insignificant we thought the visit was going to be.
As we wait in the office, in walks the doctor; a short, well-dressed, cute little woman by the name of Aliya. She introduces herself and shakes me and Tonia's hands. Our eyes are locked and she cuts to the chase.

"How are you?"

I smile and say, "I'm fine. How are you?"

Staying in character, she directs the questions back to me. "What did your doctor tell you about your cancer?"

"He told me I would have to do radiation, but no chemo." My eyes begin to search hers for reassurance that what I had been told was still the case.

She opens up my file and moves close to me and Tonia; showing us up close and personal what's on my chart.

"Your cancer is not estrogen produced. You have triple negative breast cancer, which is the most aggressive form of breast cancer anyone can have; and the hardest to fight."

A lump forms in my throat and I swallow hard before speaking.

"Will I have to have my breast removed?"

"No. Your type of cancer is so aggressive, removing your breast would not do any good because the chances of it spreading to another part of your body are so great." She tries to be as compassionate as she can while making sure I understood what she was saying.

"Ok. Ok. I hear what you are saying, but what does that mean exactly?"

"YOU HAVE TO DO CHEMO!" She says.

I sat down and just looked at her allowing her words to sink deep into my head. I could feel Tonia's hand on my back, but I felt empty inside like something had been ripped out of me. Still trying to remain strong, I look at my doctor and said, "WHY?"

Using the tip of the ink pen she tried to explain.

"Your cancer is small--very little--but so aggressive. I've seen ladies die from it; I want you to start chemo ASAP!"

UGH! It's a week from Christmas!

"Dr. Aliya, will my hair fall out?"

She looks at me and spares me the sugar coated, watered-down version of the truth.

"Yes, you will lose all of your hair."

Instantly it hits me like a ton of bricks.

I HAVE CANCER!

ME.

I HAVE CANCER, AND IM GOING TO BE BALD!

Tonia tries to make me feel better and says, "It's just hair, it will grow back."

Easy for her to say when she will have a full head of hair when I'm bald like an old man. I don't respond to either of them.

For the entire ride home I cried; calling my dad and boyfriend, giving them the news. I explain to them, as I try to absorb it myself that I have to undergo chemo! Not to mention that I can't work because chemo drains your body of white blood cells. Thus, I will have a low white blood cell count which affects my immune system's ability to fight off infection, so I can't take a chance of getting cut at work.

I can't work AND I am going to be bald! I can't stop the trail of tears from falling.

My sister takes me home. I feel like I'm dreaming. How can I have cancer? I'm the healthiest person I know!

"Lonnie, you don't feel like going to a party do you?" My sister asks me.

"I already have my outfit planned out, let me lay down and take this all in for a moment then see how I feel in a couple hours."

She kisses me and says she loves me and that everything is going to be ok, and deep down inside I believe her.

I go home and just think and think some more. I can't really say I was sad. Shock is a better description of what I feel. Try as hard as I do, I can't lay down for a nap because my mind is racing.

Lord, I have too much to do to die, so I guess I have a
fight on my hands and I'm ready for it!

"Hurry up Tonia and Kim Littlejohn because I'm ready to go the party!" I have my outfit all laid out and I stare into the mirror.

Wow, I don't look like I have cancer! I start to smile. I'm

ready to have some fun and I hope and pray that I don't get wimpy and start crying and ruin everyone's fun.

I get my emotions in check and we head to the party; it's packed. I'm having a nice time with Tonia and my friend Kim. The cares of the world of cancer are behind me for the moment. We laugh and take pictures. Suddenly the music stops and my friends Bobo and Sean are on the mic. Then I see the performer of the night stand up and it looks like they are presenting her with flowers.

"I'm going to take her flowers, they are pretty." I say to my sister as we watch the presentation.

Then I hear Sean say, "Lonnie can you come up here please?"

I tell myself that if he tries to play a joke on me I'm going to punch him in his stomach!

As I approach the stage he tells the crowd, "This is our friend Lonnie and she is battling breast cancer and is about to undergo chemo; if it can happen to her it can happen to any of you."

I feel my eyes filling up with water. I tell myself, *don't you dare cry you big punk.* I see the look of sympathy in the eyes of the crowd. I think to myself, *no don't feel sorry for me, I'm going to be fine.* I hug Bobo and Sean and tell the ladies in the crowd, "Please get checkups." When I begin to feel my voice crack, I hand the microphone back to Sean and head back to the bar to get my glass of wine. I'm stopped at least fifteen times along the way from people wanting to hug and take pictures with me. I meet a lady before I reach the bar who tells me that she is battling breast cancer too, but unlike my situation, no one talks about it. She smiles and says how much she admires my strength.

Right then I make a vow to myself to share my testimony with everyone I come in contact with. I want everyone in the same situation as me to know my struggle and to know that they are not alone. I begin to smile and become happy that I didn't let my news keep me from coming out to the party. I leave the party knowing the Lord's going to use me and my situation to encourage others while drawing me closer to Him.

Staring up at the sky I say, "Ok, Lord, give me the strength to go through this without breaking down and losing my mind."

As night approaches, I lay wide awake with my thoughts. *Will treatment hurt? How will I look bald? What if they can't get all the cancer? How am I going to look? How will people treat me?* In the midst of my thoughts, I find myself getting sleepy and soon I begin to doze off. This is the first night of many to come that tears and thoughts will end my nights.

******

It's December 25th . The kids, my family and I all have a nice time eating, opening gifts, and enjoying each other's company. But there's a feeling in the air and no one wants to say anything to mess up the moment. Everyone knew I was starting chemo in three days, and as long as I didn't mention it, neither would they. The next three days passed with a haze around them. I got on the computer and read any and everything I could on triple negative cancer and stories from other women who were battling cancer. Some say, *ignorance is bliss*; I refused to let that be my frame of mind for the battle ahead of me. I insisted on being educated about the enemy that was attacking my body. Knowledge and my faith in God would be my sword and shield. My mind finds peace in that war plan.

Before I know it, it's the night before chemo and for some reason I'm not scared at all. Instead of fear, curiosity controls my mind. All I can think about is what will happen, will it hurt, what side effects will occur, and how long before I'm bald. Other than that, I'm ready to get it started and over with!

Q: WHAT DO YOU NEED TO MOVE FORWARD?

My Friend Kim Littlejohn Tricked
Me Into Going To A Party

My Fight

Begins

Ding! Ding!

12-27-2009

> *It's Sunday night, I start chemo in the morning. I have been up reading everything I possibly can about what I'm about to go through, what to eat, and what to expect. I'm ready to start and get healthy and be there for someone when they need me. I feel loved and blessed to know that so many people love and are praying for me. I love the Lord with all my heart, and know He loves me. And I know He is going to see me through. I'm getting a second chance with it. I'm going to start doing some things and stop doing some things. Life is short and I'm going to take advantage of it.*

> *Goodnight! Going to bed...gotta start chemo 2morrow. Holla!*

It's December 28th, 2009. I walk into the *Kansas City Cancer Center* to start the fight of my life. My sister, Tonia, is with me and my sister Greta. They lead me into the chemo room where I see a lot of chairs with people sitting with IVs in their arms or in the ports that are surgically placed in their chest. I say this now and will continue to say this, "I HATE NEEDLES. HATE, HATE, HATE THEM!

They insert the IV into my arm; the first bag is a saline solution to flush my veins, then a bag of *Benadryl*, then two bags of chemo drugs. It takes about four hours to go through the whole process.

> *Ugh! I'm ready to go home. CANCER SUCKS! The Benadryl has made me sleepy. I want to go home and lay in my own bed.*

I awake the next day a little sore. My mouth is dry as cotton and the medicine is making my throat hurt. I force myself to get out of the house because my son is stressing me out and the doctor has warned me that my body is fighting to get well and stress is *not* my friend. I don't have any classes since it's the holiday; but my plans are to do classes for one hour a day. No matter how sick and tired I am I need a sense of normalcy in my life. I refuse to let cancer take away working out and training my clients.

UGH! I hate having no energy.

It's 5:00 a.m. and yet I can't make myself get up out of bed until noon. My sister Tonia comes by and makes me get out of the house. Have I mentioned I love her with everything in me, and hate for her to worry about me? Her dedication to making me feel ok makes me want to fight even harder.

Days go by and soon it's New Year's Eve. My friends came over. I cooked for them and we have a nice time, but I caution myself not to overdo it but my warning comes too late I get a horrible headache that hurts so bad that all I can do is sit on the floor in front of the toilet in the bathroom. The pain is so horrific—before I know it, I throw up.

Oh gosh, what's wrong with me? I cry and begin to frantically pray. My boyfriend is nowhere to be found, so I call Tonia, who calls the doctor followed by a call to my boyfriend telling him to get his butt home. The doctor lets me take a pain pill and says that I'm over doing it, and to take it easy because headaches are not side effects of chemo.

HAPPY NEW YEARS TO ME!

As I lay in bed consumed with my thoughts, I pray that I get the lesson I'm supposed to learn from all of this. Never once do I say, "WHY ME?" I just want to fight to get well and move forward with my life!

New Year's Day sneaks up on me. I get up, fix breakfast for my kids and my boyfriend. I'm determined to make sure that their lives are the same as they always have been. I go through the motions as best I can.

I haven't been able to have a bowel movement since I began chemo, so now on top of all the other medications that I am taking, I have to pop stool softeners as well. I feel myself getting a little down from the reality of day to day life. I used to be able to work out for two hours and now twenty minutes on the elliptical seems like an hour. I reach for a book on comfort and I try to read it. *It helps, but barely. It sure would make it easier if I had some kinda support at home, but that is a luxury that I don't have.* Mentally I make a note to myself of the observation that my son can't take seeing me like this. He stays away a lot and I know why but I can't blame him. My boyfriend is here physically; but mentally he might as well be somewhere else because he really doesn't talk to me. He just sits and texts on his phone all night as if he would rather be any place other than by my side. I need air, so I get in my truck and go for a ride in my pajamas. Driving in circles on a route to nowhere in particular, hours pass before I find myself right back at home where I started.

Before I know it, I call Brother Johnny and Pastor Newton for prayer because emotionally I'm having a hard time. In my heart I know I'm going to beat this cancer thing, but it's still hard going through it. I know I have support from friends and family and kids who love me so much, but sometimes I still feel weak.

My daughter looks at me and says, "Mommy, are you going to die?" I hate to see the fear in her eyes.

"Momma is going to be fine. I just gotta go through this in order to get better." As I say the words I realize I am saying them for her benefit and mine. I can only hope that they make us both feel better.

Before I got cancer, I was busy working day after day at *Ford*, doing my fitness classes, and taking care of my kids and my mom. That's how life was as I knew it. Now I'm not working. I'm at home barely able to make it through a day without throwing up. For more hours in a day than I care to count, I'm tired. I want to get up and do the things that normal people do, want to get up but the chemo has me drained.

I say to the Lord, "What do you want from me?"

He says, "Make time for me."

I gather some books together and try to be obedient: "Can you stand to be blessed" by T.D. Jakes; "8 Steps to Create the Life You Want" by Creflo A. Dollar; and "Landmines in the Path of the Believer" by Charles F. Stanley; along with some of Joyce Meyer's books, just anything that I think will help me grow spiritually.

I remember the doctor's words that my hair would start falling out about three weeks after I started chemo. Well, it's been two weeks and I find myself constantly checking my hair to see if it's begun falling out yet, even though I know it's going to happen. It's inevitable. Try as I might, there's nothing you can do to prepare yourself for that moment. You just have to suffer in agony knowing that one day it will happen. To prepare me for what it will look like and to prove that hair doesn't make up who you are, my sister Tonia shaved her head. Wow, I can't believe she did that. I love her for doing it, but I don't think I would have shaved my head if the table was turned.

As I lay in the bed I ask the Lord, "Please give me at least one hour a day to instruct fitness classes." I hope that I am not asking for too much, but I ask anyway. I figure it can't help to ask; I just might get it and right now, that is all I need.

Yes, I would love to know what I can do to prevent cancer from returning in my body. Yes, it's tough to make my mind tell my body to get up and workout and smile. But guess what? That's what I'm going to do! My mind is made up and ain't nothing you can do to stop a made-up mind. I'm determined to prove that.

DING, DING, THE FIGHT IS ON!

I get up, get dressed, go in the basement and force myself to do 100 pushups, four sets of 25 repetitions, then twenty-five minutes of cardio. Yes, it's tough, but I find a way to get through it. Now I'm ready to do my class. I laugh as I observe the looks on my client's faces when I walk in and say, "What's up y'all?"

As the words leave my mouth, my friend Kim Littlejohn says, "Aw hell y'all, ain't nothing changed!"

Q: HAVE YOU LET YOUR CIRCUMSTANCES CHANGE YOU?

I Would Carry My Sister On My Back If I Had To

12-28-09

Did chemo 2day, it took three hours. It wasn't bad; but the Benadryl made me really tired. Just came home and ate a little and went to sleep.

12-29-09

Woke up a little sore, took medications and ate a little. I later got outta the house for a little while and let my son stress me out. Not good at all. My mouth is dry and my throat is sore. The medication is making my lips chapped. Other than that, I'm just a little tired. I don't want to be bothered 2day; it's not a good day okay? My friend from work and her daughter came over. My sister Tonia loves me so much...I don't want to worry her. My mouth is so dry it feels like cotton!

12-30-09

Got out the house 2day. I woke up at 5:00 a.m. and couldn't make myself get up till noon. I hate having no energy. I went and ate with my sister. I love my sister so much; she is my shoulder to lean on. I ate today and drank plenty of fluids. I don't feel too bad, just tired and sluggish. I talked to Brother Johnny and Pastor Newton 2day and it helped. I'm not upset and confused, I just want to fight and get better and go on with my life and help someone else with what I've been through. I am more than a conqueror!

12-31-09

Lesa, Marsha, and DaDa came over. I cooked crab legs and I felt pretty good, just tired and kinda sore. Had a horrible headache, the pain was so bad like someone was kicking me in my head! I prayed and cried. Doctor said I could take a pain pill. I went to sleep until the New Year. Tonia was worried, I hate worrying her. I had to take care of me, I hate feeling this tired, no energy.

HAPPY NEW YEARS!

01-01-10

Got up and fixed breakfast. Still haven't been able to go to restroom. Tried to work out for twenty minutes, it seemed like an hour. Going to try and do more tomorrow. Feel kinda sluggish and sore. My dad came by today. He's worried about me. I hate seeing him worry about me! I'm about to try and read a book on comfort. John made me mad; I went for a drive in my pajamas. Still haven't been able to go to the restroom.

01-02-10

I'm about to do some pushups. Camilla and Cheryl came over to visit. Later me and John watch a movie. He texts the whole time we are together, so I get mad and go to sleep. My friend Buffy came over. She didn't comb her hair or put on makeup...LOL. She wanted to look bad because I said I did. She brought me soup...yum yum! And Tonia cut her hair off 2day. My hair hasn't fell out yet. She is so supportive. I just love her to death.

01-03-10

Smoke woke me and John up, so we went and ate breakfast. I felt a bit energized from breakfast, so I did the elliptical for twenty-five minutes and did 100 pushups. Oh, yay! I felt pretty good. I washed and folded clothes. Going to take a nap, then cook dinner and read. To GOD be the glory, great things He has done!

Rocking Another Cute Head Scarf
With My Nephew Billy

And The Side Effects Begin

It's time to get my daughter up for school but I'm drained so I coach her from my bed.

"Get your clothes on and brush your teeth. Baby if you come over to the bed, I will comb your hair."

"I can brush it." She says.

I feel horrible not getting up and seeing her off to school. But this has become a normal routine for us. As she leaves I can't help thinking that she has to be the most mature nine year old on the planet! I hear the door close behind her and promise myself I will be up with dinner waiting when she gets out of school.

My phone rings constantly and the texts won't stop coming in. *Dang, don't they know I have cancer? I'm trying to feel sorry for myself, why are they bothering me?*

I get up and force myself to eat, go to the restroom, take the dozen or so meds that I have to take, and get back in bed.

WHO THE HELL IS BEATING ON THE DOOR!

I get up. I'm pissed! They keep coming by without calling or they call and when I won't answer, they just show up. *UGH!*

Who is it this time? I look out the blinds and my heart sinks, it's my daughter. *Damn, I slept all day! How did that happen?*

"Hi mom." She says without a care in the world. "You still sleep?"

"Yeah, kind of Trin; how was your day?"

"Fine. You said you was coming to eat lunch with me today; what happened?"

"I'm so sorry...momma slept all day." Instantly I feel a sense of shame.

"It's ok." She says with a smile that lights up the room. I love this little girl and I vow to eat lunch with her once a week.

Time to change my ways. Like I said before, nothing stops a made-up mind. I shower, get dressed and go do my fitness class. Not only do I want to let my clients see that if I can come to class every day and train them despite battling cancer, then they have no excuse to stay healthy despite what life is tossing their way. They can either complain and give up, or complain and do something about it. The choice is theirs to make, my only goal is to be the best example I can be.

I feel like I am making progress with my clients, but I can't say the same thing for the men in my life. My son and I constantly argue or we don't talk to each other at all, and more times than not, he stays away from home altogether. My boyfriend calls daily from work to see if I'm okay or if I need anything. But when he walks in the house all I get is a, "How do you feel?" Once I answer, that's it. No further conversation. *Wow! Never have I felt so alone in my life.* Again I grab my keys and go for a ride...in my pajamas.

I do this a lot. I've never been the type to cry on anyone's shoulder. So instead I ride around in my car and cry. I cry until my tears enable me to see where I'm going.

Lord I need you, what do you want me to do?

Draw closer to me He says.

Ok, ok. I got it! I'll stop thinking that it's all about Lonnie!

I'm beginning to learn the lesson. Working at *Ford* for all these years, doing my fitness classes, taking care of my kids, catering to my boyfriend, and hanging with my friends; THE LORD WANTED MY ATTENTION. What better way to get it then to touch my health—the very thing I strive to take care of— that part of my core that signified who I was...at least in my mind.

So many times we think that what we go through is

for us, when reality is that most of the time our trials are for those around us; the ones who are watching, saying, "I see her smiling and always trying to encourage others; let's see how she's going to handle this."

I finally get it. His lesson is now abundantly clear.

I make up my mind that no matter how I feel or what I am going through with my chemo—the problems with dealing with my son and my emotionally absent boyfriend—no matter how any of that makes me feel, once I leave the four walls of my home I will have a smile on my face and tell of my blessing and not complain. I realize now that this cancer is not a curse; it's a blessing in disguise.

The doctor said it would be about three weeks after chemo before my hair started falling out. Well, guess what? It's been three weeks and I ain't going to sit around and wait for it to happen. So I get my dreads cut off and my hair shaved down to a cute low cut like a little boy. I look in the mirror and it's not that bad. I still look like Lonnie.

After I Shaved My Head

*****

01-04-10

I woke up and cooked breakfast. I went grocery shopping. I wore my mask, and I got my head shaved today. Everyone liked it. I cooked dinner and did my class today for an hour. I felt pretty good, and stayed at my mom's house. Let's see how long I stay in bed 2morrow morning, LOL. I can do all things through Christ that strengthens me!

Brother Johnny and Sister Gwen called and prayed for me 2day. Call me bold, but I'm going to beat this!

01-05-10

Slept pretty good stayed in the bed until about 10:00 a.m. went and got a one-hour massage, it was wonderful. I made sure I stayed woke to enjoy it. I came home and relaxed, I went and did my class for an hour and felt pretty good. I worked out for the whole hour. My appetite is pretty good, I eat a decent portion, just try not to snack on junk food. Came home and took a shower. I took pictures with my shaved head. I look pretty hot. I must say so myself.

God is Awesome. He keeps on blessing little ole sinful me!

01-07-10

I felt like a bum! I didn't do anything but sleep and eat. I didn't leave the house. I didn't take a shower or do anything. LOL, I was a bum 2day!

My sister wanted me to feel special so she told me to come over for a photo shoot! *Have I mentioned that I love her and she is my best friend?* I take all kinds of outfits, sunglasses, and makeup. I'm so excited, this is so fun, and for the next couple of hours I forget I have cancer. I'm smiling. I'm laughing, and the pictures are beautiful. I begin to notice that my sister was right; my hair doesn't make me who I am. I'm much more than a few strands of hair.

Yeah, that's what I think and feel until two days later when I scratch my head and my hair comes off in my hand. *Aw hell, it's coming out!* I knew it would happen eventually and prepared myself a little by cutting my hair off to prevent from losing my dreads one by one. But somehow that wasn't enough. Nothing can really prepare you for when your hair is shedding off in your hand and the spots are as bare as a baby's bottom, or as bald as an old man. So the hair cut, that I thought was so cute, has spots in it now. I resort to wearing scarves and say a special thanks to my friend who gave me a scarf party as soon as the doctor informed me that I would have to undergo chemo.

Thank God for small blessings.

Life goes on. I do my classes and hangout with my friends; I go to church and do everything else I want to do; except now I do it with my head covered.
*****

It's time for my second bout of chemo. I have to go every three weeks until I have four rounds complete.

UGH! I hate needles. Hate, Hate, Hate!

The routine is much the same as the first time, only slightly different. First they give me my chemo; two different kinds. I stay for three and half hours and then I have to give blood.

Are you serious? Why is all of this even necessary?

I wait to talk to the nurse about my results. She informs me my white blood count is 0.0, which means I have no immune system and can't fight off any kind of infections. She informs me not to be around a lot of people, and if I have to interact with people, I have to wear a mask.

What? All I can do is sigh out loud as I listen to instructions and figure out a way to follow them.

For the next couple of days I do my classes and try not to get close to anyone, shake hands or do anything that will put me at risk. But that didn't last long before I was hugging, laughing, and talking not only to my clients, but also people in *Walmart* and everywhere else I went.

LORD, PLEASE PROTECT ME. YOU KNOW I'M HARD-HEADED AND FRIENDLY."

I've had two bouts of chemo, with two more to go. I haven't lost all my hair yet. It kind of looks like *Fire Marshall Bill* on "In Living Color" so I never take my scarf off, not even at home unless I'm alone. I don't want my kids to feel uneasy, and I don't want my boyfriend to be turned off. It's bad enough that I can't hold my bladder because of the all the medicine making my kidneys and liver work overtime, now I'm going bald too. I want him to at least be still attracted to me so the scarves never come off.

I must admit, I'm still not angry, nor do I even feel the need to question God, "Why me?" Instead I say to the Lord, "Please use me to encourage others and give me strength when I'm weak to carry me on with a smile on my face."

My Daddy Telling A Story About Me At A Head Scarf Party

*****

It's been almost a week since I have seen my son. I'm not sure where he is, but I know I can't fight stress and fight to stay well at the same time. I love him with every fiber of my being but I chose to fight to get well. I ask the Lord to watch over him and protect him where ever he might be. I turn him over to the Lord, and set my focus on battling cancer and being there for my daughter, whom I know must be scared and misses the time we used to spend together.

I'm officially completely bald. The little hair that was there I washed off in the shower tonight. I stare and look in the mirror for so long that I lose track of time. My head is shaped cute, not like a cone head. I'm thankful for that small piece of grace on my behalf. I look like an *M&M*. I just rub my head and stare; then I rub it some more.

Dang, I guess I really do have cancer.

Reality sinks in again. I look in the mirror and say, "Lonnie, you have cancer, but it doesn't have you!" I resolve that no matter how it turns out, I'm going to live my life to the fullest. I remind myself that nothing can stop a made-up mind, and then I tie my head up because my boyfriend hasn't seen me completely bald yet.

With my scarf tied tightly in place, I say my prayers and get in the bed, but that does not stop the Devil from putting strange thoughts in my head. Some nights are harder than others and I have to shake my head so hard to get them out.

What if you don't beat breast cancer? What if you die? You should take all those pills and get it over with now.

The thoughts run ramped in my mind as I try to shake them off.

DEVIL YOU ARE A LIE! Stop trying to take me out because

once I beat this, and you know I will, I'm going to be stronger and tell the whole world my story!

To make sure I didn't get any crazy ideas and to remove some of the Devil's power, I moved the medicine from on the table close to my bed to the dresser on the other side of the room. I figured by the time I could get up enough energy to walk clear over to the other side of the room, hopefully that would be enough time to talk myself out of doing something crazy.

People battling cancer are awake with their thoughts. When we don't want to think, we think. When we are tired of thinking, we think. Whether it's good or bad thoughts...we are thinking.

I've begun trying harder to use that time to read whatever I can get my hands on, entertaining myself on the computer, praying or making up workouts. An idle mind can be the Devil's playground so I make sure there is no room in my sandbox for him.

And when all that fails, I pop a sleeping pill and go to sleep. Yeah, yeah, yeah, it's easy for you to say I shouldn't use that cop out, but when you are tired of thinking, what else can you do?

Q: HAVE YOUR THOUGHTS CONSUMED YOU? WHAT DID YOU DO?

Out And About With My New Shiny Shirt

*****

01-08-10

I'm going bowling at 10. Then I'm going to the doctor to get my white blood count and me and Tonia are going out to eat. This is my last day taking my meds until my next bout of chemo! January 2nd at 1:30 my white blood count was 0.0. Yep it couldn't be any lower. It's Friday and I have to stay in the house until Monday. I'm going to stay at Tonia's because I don't like John. I can't wait until the Lord sends me an honest, faithful man. I had a ball bowling 2day, I bowled a 146, Yep!

01-19-10

Haven't wrote in a while...been trying to stay busy. Tonia has been getting me out. I luv her and Matt, they do so much for me. I have a friend who helps me out emotionally, he doesn't seem to care that I don't have any hair and he always tells me how beautiful I am. He talks and listens to me and he is just as caring as I am. I wish I could take his qualities and put them in John. I'm getting new tires plus getting my oil changed. Life goes on. My son stresses me out so much. I'm going to have to just give him to the Lord. I have to cut back on my eating. I have turned into a pig. LOL

01-21-10

I went to court with John over Korey. He is such a BUTT hole. Had my class today and my stomach is getting big for real it is. I do my second bout of chemo 2morrow. I'm ready to get it over with and go on with my life.

GOD IS GOOD!

What? More Side Effects?

I resume my everyday activities. Man I wish I could go to work! I need an outlet. Everyone is at work during the day. I'm lonely and wish I could join the rest of the work force. I read and write, and stay on the computer. I have never sat this still and watched this much TV in my life. I force myself to get up every morning. I go to *Patsy's Coffee Shop* and get my white chocolate caramel latte and ride around visiting people. I've never been the type to just sit around, so no need to start now!

I've gotten good at making sure I'm out of bed when my baby gets out of school, and usually I have dinner ready. I'm completely bald now. I still look the same, just kind of like a cute bald lady. But now all my hair is gone; from my head, eyebrows, eyelashes, hair on my legs, all of it...every last piece of hair on my body is gone! Even the hair on my private area and my nose hair! My fingernails have turned black. I've lost a toenail and broke two teeth in the back. I feel like the man in the movie, *"The Fly" only I'm better looking.*

I don't want anyone to dare feel sorry for me. It could be worse. At least the teeth fell out in the back and not in the front. If it were the other way around, I would have a real problem! But then again, I always wanted *Veneers*!

I meet so many ladies at the Cancer Center that seem so withdrawn, so sad. I make it a point to always go to the chemo room with a smile, and I talk to everyone in there. I even wake the ones up that are sleep! I have my mind made up, I'm on a mission. Yes, I have cancer; but cancer doesn't have me. I have no problem wrapping my head and getting out. It is encouraging to people that know what I am going through to see me out with a smile on my face. Some cannot believe I am battling cancer. I remember this one lady that begged me to take my hood off just to prove to her I that I didn't have any hair.

I told her, "No. I won't do that. Who would lie about having cancer and being bald?"

Her response was, "You look so good it's hard to believe you have cancer."

I would have believed that coming from someone else; but this particular lady just wanted to see me bald for her own sense of enjoyment. You'd be surprised at the people that like being negative and want to bring others down with them.

"No girl. Get out of my face! Cancer or not, I'm still Lonnie. Please don't make me prove it to you."

My hair was not the only source of amusement for some people. I've never been a big fan of makeup, and my friend Sean got a kick out of wiping my eyebrows off, after I had drawn them on, just because he said one was always crooked. It's nothing like having friends that refuse to treat you any different just because you're sick.

I'm growing closer to the Lord and asking Him daily for guidance. I need to know what He wants from me.

What lesson am I to get from all this?

I'm trying not to stress between doctor appointments and taking care of home. It's also hard not really hearing from my son, and hearing my boyfriend complain about my friends and sisters always being at the house.

HELLO, I HAVE CANCER! And no support or help at home!

What the hell am I supposed to do?

I NEED TO MAKE SOME CHANGES!

Q: ARE YOU LETTING THINGS STRESS YOU?

HOW ARE YOU GOING TO CHANGE IT?

My Niece Kiesha Loves This Wig Because She Thinks It Makes
Us Look Alike

01-24-10

It's the Sunday after the second round of chemo and physically I'm ok, just a little tired emotionally. It's hard just thinking about my situation and thinking someone should act in a different way, and they don't. In the end, I know the Lord is in control and everything is going to be ok. It's just going through the hard and lonely times when I say, "Lord help me." I don't say why to Him. I just say, "Lord give me strength." I went to Christ Temple 2day, it's been nights when Brother Johnny has helped me more than he knows. It's a learning and humbling experience to have to lean on people. This is new for me.

I CAN DO ALL THINGS THROUGH CHRIST WHICH STRENGTHENS ME!

02-01-10

I had a pretty good day 2day. I'm constantly praying for the Lord to touch my mind. You'd be surprised the thoughts that come across my mind. I have a little hair left, I'm going to wash it 2night and see if the rest of it will come out. I just want to use this experience to help someone else make their journey easier. Let them see Christ in me despite my condition.

Be Careful What You Ask For!

I'M ALMOST DONE WITH CHEMO!

I have one more treatment to go then eight weeks of radiation every day. The side effects have lightened up, all except I have thrash in my mouth which makes all food hard to eat because my mouth and tongue are raw. I drink protein shakes because I refuse to lose weight. Yes, I'm sick. Yes, I have cancer, but that doesn't mean I have to look sick. See I made up my mind that if I think positive thoughts, I will have positive outcomes. So from now on, I say to myself that I only want positive people around me.

To turn my thoughts into reality, I pray and say, "Lord, surround me with positive people, and anyone that has my best interest at heart or is ready to deal with me at the next level you are about to take me to. Remove all negative people from my life!"

Let me fore warn you; don't pray this prayer unless you are sure you will be able to handle the outcome.

It seems like in a three-week span, a friend that I normally hang out with and talk to almost every day has all of a sudden stopped contacting me. They no longer visit, text or call and they know I am battling cancer. Anyone who knows me knows that I don't bother with anyone who doesn't want to be bothered. Needless to say, that friendship has gone by the waste side. I take that to mean that God is answering my prayers by removing negative people from my life; I'm getting exactly what I prayed for even though I did not know it when I asked. But that is not the only thing that happened after my prayer. My son has also moved out of my house and moved in with his girlfriend, and not only is my boyfriend cheating, but he is planning on leaving me for another woman.

WOW Lord, I guess you let things happen the way You

see fit, not the way that is comfortable or easy for us.

Yes, I'm hurt even though things weren't right with my boyfriend. A woman knows when something isn't right, but I'm fighting for my life. I am not trying to stress and worry about what someone is, or isn't doing. And like I said, "I'm not going to bother anyone that doesn't want to be bothered."

So I'm bald and not working. My son's gone and my guy is leaving but has the nerve to ask can he stay until he finds another place.

Yeah, I know what you're thinking...*HELL NAWH, PUT HIS ASS OUT. THROW HIS STUFF ON THE FRONT LAWN AND PUNCH HIM IN THE STOMACH!*

That's what I should say, but instead I say, "Ok. You can stay until you find somewhere to stay." Then I look him straight in the eyes and ask, "Why do you do me like this? No, I'm not perfect, but I'm a good lady and I'm easy to talk, so you don't have to stay with me because I have cancer. It's stopped me from doing nothing!"

Of course I didn't get an answer from him, and since I'm not working, an extra month of rent from him would be great in helping the ends meet; so I just leave it all alone. Although I'm hurt, I'm so focused on finding my answer from the Lord that I'm not letting anything keep me down. It's strange how in the midst of the storm, you can still have peace. But that's exactly what I have. PEACE OF MIND.

Yeah, it still hurts. Yes, I still cry, and of course, I still have my insecurities. But I cry and hurt inside my home, because when I leave the house it's not about how Lonnie's feeling, it's about what I can do or say to encourage others, or make their day a little better or bring a smile to their face. And guess what? If that means forgetting about me and my problems for

a while, then so be it. Most of the time I'm smiling and so full of joy, talking and laughing, I forget about my situation and then have to ask myself, "Why in the hell are you so happy?"
YES, I TALK TO MYSELF. AND GUESS WHAT? I EVEN ANSWER MYSELF SOMETIMES!

I tell myself how many people would love to get a second chance in life. No, I can't go back and change the things that I have done, but I can surely do something differently and not take life, or the people around me, for granted. I'm so thankful for my family and friends. How lonely my battle would be if I had to go through this alone. I feel sorry for the people I see at the Cancer Center who sit and receive their treatment week after week alone; with no one by their side. I can reach out to them. I try to as often as I can.

As I am at the Cancer Center I see an older lady that catches a taxi to and from the Cancer Center for her treatments, so I ask her, "May I give you a ride home?"

She says, "No, I like catching a cab and don't like bothering anyone for a ride."

I see myself in this lady; so independent that you don't want to ask anyone for help even though you need it. This is definitely another eye opener for me. I vow to stop thinking I can do everything alone, and tell myself that there's nothing wrong with asking and accepting help when you need it. It's ironic how many time I thought that since I've done everything on my own; paid my bills, raised my kids, took care of my household and everything that goes along with those things, that asking for help would make me needy or weak. In my eyes, it didn't matter that I have cancer. I just didn't want anyone to think I was needy. I felt that way until I saw that older lady, weak from chemo, barely able to walk, having trouble getting in and out of a cab, yet refusing my help.
From that moment on I tell myself that I won't be like that.

59

I can't wait for someone to ask what I need. From now on, I'm sure going to tell them!

Q: ARE YOU TO PROUD TO ASK FOR HELP?

Sean And Tonia In The Chemo Room

*****

02-02-10

I didn't get out much 2day; pretty much slept in all day. I did wash some clothes and clean up a little bit. I had a good work out. Working out gives me something to look forward to. Starting tomorrow I'm going to really start watching what I eat. I want to be healthy as I can. I'm about to read and go to bed. I know the Lord is going to use me. He is just getting me ready.

02-18-10

Haven't wrote in a while. I've had good and bad days. I still can't believe I have cancer. It's like, WOW, I have cancer. Me. Lonnie. I have cancer. Life is strange and you have to trust everything happens for a reason. GOD knows what He is doing. I luv GOD, I'm not mad at him, I just ask that He keep me and strengthen me.

Last Chemo! Oh Yeah!

03-05-10

Oh, Yeah! Oh, Yeah! I did my last chemo treatment today. My friends: Sean, Bobo, Myke and my sister Tonia went with me. I start radiation in three weeks. I'm ready to get on with my life. God is awesome and I love and trust Him with all my heart.

TO GOD BE THE GLORY!

Even when we don't understand, just trust that HE will do what you trust Him to do.

AMEN!

Out With The Girls While Rocking My Favorite Head Scarf

I wake up early, excited like the kids are on the last day of school. It's my last chemo session today. Wow, I can't believe it's over. Well, I still have eight weeks of radiation, but sitting for four hours with a needle in my arm is over!

I get up; put my scarf on, my jeans, and my heels. Yes, I always dress up at all my doctor appointments. Like I said, "You don't have to look sick just because you have cancer! "So I always put my makeup on, dress to impress with heels, matching purse and scarf. It makes the nurses' smile and the patients as well to see me so full of energy. My sisters: Greta and Tonia, my friends: Bobo, Sean and Michael are meeting me at the Cancer Center for my last chemo session. We are all so happy; it's been a long road and I'm ready to get it over with. I walk in the Cancer Center full of joy and words for everyone. I walk in the chemo room and hear a lady talking, not only louder than I would, but more than I would.

HOLD UP! What's going on? Who's that?

It's my first time meeting Karen, she is battling breast cancer too; and boy can she talk a lot. She's so confident and reminds me of myself. It's my last day of treatment, but she isn't finished with her treatments yet. We talk and exchange numbers because it's good to surround yourself with positive people.

I sit with my IV in my arm left arm because I can never use my right arm to give blood or even get my blood pressure taken because I had my lymph nodes removed. It's like it's dead or at least useless in that regard. I look around and watch all the people receiving treatments; and focus on all my friends and my sisters. I get emotional thinking back on my journey, how it started, what I have gone through, all the support I've had and all the support I didn't have.

Thank you JESUS, for keeping me even when at times I didn't want to be kept.

I think about all the friends I have made here, and how nice the nurses are. I finish my last chemo and the nurses come and bring me a certificate and some balloons. They really aren't balloons, but blown up examination gloves with bandages hanging for the strings. I get my picture taken with Sean and Bobo and I'm so happy. So happy!

THANK YOU JESUS! One part down; and one to go.

They wrap my arm and I look around at all the people that still have treatments left. I get sad. I walk around and hug everyone, telling them to keep fighting. No, I don't know these people personally, but I love them and I relate to their struggle. Fighting for your life is a hard, long fight and you want to win. So you're going to give it everything you have. I will never forget the sad empty feeling I had as I turned to walk out of the chemo room leaving them behind, and praying that I never have to sit in those chairs again. I only want to enter the room if I'm coming to say, "Hi."

My friend and sisters hug me, and we walk out of the Cancer Center. Yes, I will be back in three weeks to start radiation, but for now I'm done and nothing can steal this joy that I'm feeling until I get home.

Q: DO YOU ALLOW OTHERS TO STEAL YOUR JOY?

With Sean And Bobo After My Last Chemo Treatment

The Truth Shall Set You Free

Although I've had my last chemo treatment, it stays in your system for three weeks. So I'm still a little tired; but I'm ready for it to leave my system so I can go to the dentist and get these teeth pulled that have broken off in my gums. I also want to get my nails done because they have turned black. Since I don't start radiation for three more weeks, I have to find something to do with my time.

I ask the Lord, "What do you want me to do? I've been reading. I've been trying to talk to YOU, so what now?"

"Talk to others." He says.

WOW Lord, I thought I was doing that. I talk to people everywhere I go.

He said, "Keep talking."

I sit and think about what the Lord told me. I call Karen, the lady I met at the Cancer Center. Unlike me, she has lost a lot of weight and wants to get stronger, so we agree to meet at a track and walk two to three times a week.

It's Sunday; I'm up getting ready for church. It's also the day John is moving out and I admit even though I knew this day was coming, it still hurts a little seeing his stuff packed and him sitting and waiting for his friend to get here with the truck to help him move. So I say, "Let me know when he gets here so that I can leave. I don't want to have to watch you load your stuff and pull off."

He says, "Ok." Nothing more; that was it. I have been waiting to ask him a question and now seems as good a time as any so I say, "Do you still love me?"

"Lonnie, I'm not going to answer that."

"Why did you cheat?"

"Lonnie, I'm not going to answer that last question.

"Is there anything you do want to say before you

70

leave?"

Without looking in my direction, he says, "We are on two different levels, it just didn't work."

Now that was a million-dollar answer. I'm moving up and don't need extra baggage. His answer was an eye opener for me. Everyone can't go where the Lord is trying to take you! With that answer, I pick up my purse and walk passed him and say, "Have your stuff out and be gone before I get home from church. Don't leave anything because there's no coming back to get anything!" As I pull out the garage I say, "Lord, you are turning me into a punk!" The old Lonnie would have thrown all his stuff in the backyard in the pool, and sold the wheels off his car! But no, I drive off headed to church, thinking, *Dang, now I'm going to be lonely.* But guess what? I was lonely when he was here with me, so really, nothing has changed.

"LORD PLEASE LET THE PASTOR HAVE A GOOD WORD
        FOR ME TODAY BECAUSE I NEED IT!"

Church was good and I am ready to get home and clear my head. As I walk in the door my house looks the same;
only thing missing was the television off the wall, and a futon mattress. I smile and say, "I'm sure glad my house was furnished before I met him." Then I get extremely happy to see all my closet space; empty and free. So many times we think we need things and people to complete us. Let me tell you, nothing in the world can compare to having peace of mind. No person or material thing can give you that. In order to have room for new things and blessings, you have to get rid of things that you had no business holding on to in the first place. With that being said, I'm about to add some blessings to these two extra closets that I have!

With two weeks left before I start radiation, I need

something to do. Everyone I know works during the day, and my daughter is in school. I decide to call Karen, from the Cancer Center, and we agree to meet at the track and go walking. She's trying to build her strength back up and she also wants to gain some weight. We walk and talk; I'm glad I met her. Although her body is weak right now, her spirit is strong! She informs me that she doesn't care what her doctors say; she trusts the Lord and whatever HIS will is for her life is okay with her. As I watch her walk and lift the weights that I brought, I get so encouraged because even though she's getting short of breath, she looks at me and in between gasping for air she says, "No, let's go around one more time." After another round I ask if she needs to take a break. Wow, how I wish more people were like her. Life is hard at times. Yes, you're going to be dealt a bad hand at times. Are you going to give in and go throw your cards in? Or are you going to trust the Lord will help you play the right one?

I had promised myself to go eat lunch every Friday with my daughter at school. One thing you have to love about kids is that they're going to say exactly what's on their mind. After noticing that I always had my head covered when I came to school, a little boy asked me, "Are you bald under there?"

I said, "Yes."

"Why?" He asks full of curiosity.

"Because I have cancer."

All of the kids look at me and I look at my daughter and smile to let her know I'm ok with him asking. I don't want her to feel the need to beat him up when I leave.

My Favorite Sweater After Losing My Hair
~ Sexy & Bald~

*****

As I start the next phase of dealing with my cancer; I have all kinds of concerns and questions about radiation, just like I had before I started chemo, so I get on the computer and read all I can about radiation. Since it's so strong, you can only do so much of it at a time. I have to go every day for eight weeks at 9:00 a.m. They say it only takes fifteen minutes. *Is that all?* Dang, I wish I could go to work. What am I going to do with myself for the rest of the day after I leave the Cancer Center? Although I think positive most of the time, I believe the Lord is going to see me through this battle. I'm still human and yes, negative thoughts enter my mind when I have too much time on my hands. I've got to come up with something to do so I'm not sitting around all day.

For the next two weeks I get up, get my daughter off to school, put my head phones on, and go walking for an hour. Then I would go home, shower, grab some coffee, and ride around visiting my friends at work, and go by my mom's house to see what she's doing. I check on her nurse to make sure she is doing what she is supposed to be doing and not mistreating my mom.

I find myself riding around a lot. Gas is high and I drive a truck, but I have to do something since I get bored easy. I really think I have ADHD or some other hyper-disorder. I know that at times it's good to just sit and think and reflect; but I have done that so much these last couple of months that I need to take a break from thinking sometimes. All my thoughts aren't positive all the time; and yes, I get scared at times.

Often I just lay awake in the bed feeling my breast where they cut the cancer out. I wonder if the cancer is gone. I'm constantly feeling and rubbing to see if I can feel another lump.

74

I know the Lord isn't the author of confusion and fear, but the human part of me gets scared at times.

Even though I've undergone radiation, I refuse to cancel any of my workout sessions. I also go to stores, the mall, hang out with my friends and anything else that I feel like doing. I get tired at times, and sometimes I have to take breaks, but for the most part I keep busy. It's important to me that anyone watching will see that if I could find the strength to move past my circumstances and push myself to stay fit with a smile on my face, then they have no excuses not to do the same.

Sometimes in life you're just going to have to play the hand you're dealt. I'm going to say it again...NOTHING CAN CHANGE A MADE-UP MIND! Nothing! Yes, times get hard and we have to deal with life's ups and downs; like bills, loss of income, failed relationships, health issues, and the deaths of loved ones. But at the end of the heartache and sorrow you have to believe that you're going to make it. You have to know that in the midst of your storm, the Lord will give you peace. I'm a witness; battling cancer, losing my hair, my teeth, not being able to work, my son acting out, and my boyfriend leaving me!

OH, BUT I HAVE PEACE AND JOY, AND I'M NOT LOSING MY MIND!

No one but Jesus can give you that kind of peace.

I can't help but think that there were people waiting to see me crack under the pressure. And guess what? I did crack at times in my house, alone at night. But when I walked out of the house, I was all smiles. You see it's when everyone around you is expecting you to crack and give up and yet they see you smiling and trusting the Lord in spite of your circumstances; that's the moment that you encourage others. There is nothing like being a blessing to others, and at the same time realizing how blessed you are. I'm thankful that the Lord loves me enough to bless little ole sinful me.

I tell everyone where ever I go, "CANCER IS NOT MY CURSE, IT WAS MY BLESSING." You don't get to choose how you're blessed; that's the Lord's job.

Q: ARE YOU TRULY READY FOR WHAT YOU'RE ASKING THE LORD FOR?

My Second Walk. My Girl Rhonda And I Are Both Survivors

Radiation (Eight Weeks... Every Day)

It's time for my second phase of treatment to begin. I have radiation every day for the next eight weeks at 9:00 a.m. I'm more curious than I am nervous or scared. I wonder if it will hurt, and will it only takes ten minutes like they informed me it would. I choose to go to the radiation alone since it's every day and doesn't take long. The doctors tell me not to use perfume or soap on the right side of my body, and they give me a clear rock looking stone to use for deodorant. Besides the wrap on my head, I look very healthy and notice how people look at me when I walk in. I know they're wondering, *does she have cancer, If so, what kind?* They are probably also wondering how old I am; because if I do say so myself, I look darn good for my age.

I walk in with my coffee in one hand and dressed like I'm going somewhere other than the Cancer Center. I love dressing up. Being bald and having cancer aren't going to change who I am.

I sit and wait on my name to be called. I look around at all the people in the room. Some are older, some are bald, some are alone, and some are with their spouses and kids. We are all here to fight for our lives!

Some look tired, some look worried. I see an older white lady that has the neatest hair, I want to touch it. I sit next to her and a lady that I later learned was her sister. The nurses call my name and I follow them out of the reception area. They weigh me and take some blood.

Have I mentioned how much I hate needles!

They give me a key to a room and a gown to put on. I have to take my shirt off and sit and wait for them to call me back to the radiation room. As I sit alone, I stare at the tattoo that the doctor had put on me two weeks earlier so that they could line me up on the same spot every day for the radiation treatment. *Ouch*, I wince remembering how much it hurt when they did it. Since I'm dark in skin color, they had to do it three times in order to be able to see the dots they tattooed on.

My name is called and I go back where the nurses are. They comment on how much they like my head wrap and how it matches my shoes.

TOLD YOU I'M SHARP!

I lay on the table, remove my gown, put my arms behind my head and take my scarf off because I can't lay my head flat because of the knot I tied in back. They line the machine up to the dots I have tattooed on my breast and down my side. Relax, they repeat over and over and I try to. The nurses left the room and said they will be back in a few minutes. Alone in the room, I stare at the machine that's going to give me the treatment I NEED TO FIGHT FOR MY LIFE! It moves up and down and the lights kind of look like a laser show with me smack dab in the middle. The lights circle about three times and then it stops and a nurse walks in

"Ok, you're all done."

Wow, it didn't hurt and it only took about seven minutes. I walked back to the room to change, thinking to myself, *dang I wish I could go to work.* The whole treatment only takes about ten minutes as promised and it's still early, what the hell am I going to do for the rest of the day?

I shift my focus to my workouts. I will use my time to make up new routines. I know my clients are ready for me to go back to work because some of these workouts I make up even I have to shake my head and say, "Lonnie, you are crazy." Then I laugh because the crazier it seems, the more I like it and I can't wait to get to class to instruct it. I love when my clients call me names and roll their eyes. I laugh at them and think to myself, *yeah, this is a good workout, I think I will keep this one!* Although they won't admit it, I know they like it too.

I continue going for my radiation and doing my classes at the house and at the community center. When I go for my treatments, I now speak to the lady with the pretty hair, and have met a man battling throat cancer. We all talk regularly. The lady with the pretty hair has her appointment right before mine, and the man with throat cancer his appointment after mine, so we see each other every day. He has two weeks left of treatment and she has three weeks left. I'm the newbie since I still have six weeks left, but you couldn't tell it because I try to stay busy and positive; and I always smile and talk to everyone whether they want me to or not.

No matter how long or bad my night is (was), I wake up and thank the Lord for a new day. I ask HIM to be in charge of thoughts, my mind, my actions, and my words. So many times we let our issues and circumstances stop us from thinking we can be a blessing to someone else. We can be a blessing to someone just by telling them what we are going through, or just smiling at someone who looks down or lonely. Believe it or not, you are not the only person in this world going through ups and downs. So no matter how bad you think you have it, I promise you can find someone that would love to trade places with you.

I have rationalized in my mind that my blessings outweigh any of my setbacks. Yes, I complain. Yes, I look at what others have and wonder when will it be my turn, especially when it's someone that has no relationship with the Lord. But I have gotten tired of being bitter and comparing myself to others because at the end of the day, what the Lord has for me is for me. It's nothing I can do to speed up the process. The Lord works on His time, not mine. Until He is ready to bless me, I'm content.

Most of us aren't ready for what the Lord wants us to have; so until then I'm going to praise HIM in advance. I'm also going to love and smile even when I don't feel like it or when I feel someone has done me wrong. I believe in the saying that what goes around comes around. So you better be careful what you give, because it will find its way back to you. Believe that. You cannot change your past, but you can work on being a better person today. Saying sorry to a person that has wronged you, or forgiving a person who has wronged you, is the first step at moving forward, and you will be surprised at how much weight is lifted off you when you do it.

Don't get me wrong, it's a constant struggle for me to excuse someone when I know darn well that they have wronged me. It upsets me more when that person acts like they have done nothing wrong. I can honestly say that I have hindered some of my blessings because I'm always saying, "Lord, why are they prospering and I'm not? Lord, when are you going to punish them for how they have treated me?" But I've changed. I've learned to put my feelings aside, and pray for them, asking the Lord to forgive me for sitting back wishing and waiting for things to happen to them.

The Lord knows how to deal with people to get their attention; even mine. When I sit back and realize that I've done a lot of things I should have been punished for and yet the Lord showed me mercy, man...it's a whole lot easier to forgive someone knowing darn well you have wronged people also. I can't throw stones unless I toss one at myself first!

Humm, did the Lord have to make me sit still

this long just for me to realize all the things I'm finally realizing about life? I just have to ask myself that question often.

I love the nurses at the Cancer Center and they love to see me coming. They say I am a ray of sunshine due to the scarves I wear. I have hundreds of scarves that were gifts from my friends and family who gave them to me when they found out I was going to lose my hair. I had two scarf parties so I really racked up. I plan on donating most of them to charity once my hair starts growing back.

My two new friends at the Cancer Center are finishing up their treatments. The man battling throat cancer gives me a box of chocolates and tells me to take care of myself. I hug him and tell him, "I never want to see you here again!" He smiles because he knows I mean it in a good way.

My friend with the neat hair gives me her phone number and I ask her, "Are you sure you don't want to trade places with me and do two more weeks of radiation?

She replies, "I love you, but no thank you. I don't want to trade places with you but you're going to be just fine."

I smile and hug her and say, "Yeah, I know."

I'm truly happy for both of them and sad at the same time. Sad because I'm never going to see them again unless we have a checkup appointment at the same time, but I'm also kind of scared for them. I hope they never have to undergo treatment again, and wish I was finished with my treatment like they are. I have done six weeks of radiation every day. My breast is burnt and is peeling really bad. The skin rubs off inside my bra and it itches and burns pretty bad. I try not to touch it because touching it makes it worse.

Three nights a week I stay at my mom's house. I have

to lift her and I try not to let her know that lifting her hurts me. I try to hide the pain, but I can tell that she sees it which makes her sad that I have to take care of her. Sometimes she cries; then I cry too. At moments like this I say, "Lord, I hate to see my mom suffer and she hates to see me suffer; please give us strength, peace, and understanding in the midst of our circumstances. I love my mom and would take care of her no matter how much pain I'm in, and I know that she would do the same for me and my brothers and sisters if the tables were turned.

I have said this before, and I will say it again..."ONCE YOU'VE MADE UP YOUR MIND TO DO SOMETHING, NOTHING CAN STOP YOU. A MADE-UP MIND IS STUBBORN!

Q: WHAT HAVE YOU MADE UP YOUR MIND TO DO?

My Brother Sean; This Is Another One Of My Favorite Hooded
Outfits

Last Week Of Radiation

I have five more days of radiation. This last part of the treatment is nothing like the first part. That chemo just zapped all of my energy! Radiation didn't make me tired at all; my skin peeled kind of bad, and my breast is (was) burnt and swollen, but at least I had some energy. Even though my breast is swollen, I sure wish the other one was the same size as this one. The radiation has made my right breast firm and hard; I wish they would have put radiation on the other side. I would have had no complaints!

My last week is no different than my first. I dress up, wrap my head, smile and talk to everyone in the waiting room. I know some of them can't wait until I'm done with treatment because I can tell my talking and happy mood gets on some of their nerves. Oh well, I said I can tell that's how they feel; I didn't say that their feelings could make me stop!

I sit down in thought and wonder how many will beat cancer. How many will have to battle it again, and how many will lose the fight. I make up in mind that I can't choose how and when I die; but I can choose to live my life to the fullest. Every morning that I wake up I'm blessed to see another day. I finish my last radiation, and the nurses gave me a certificate of completion. Now I have to wait three weeks to see if the cancer is gone and if I will be able to say, "I'm cancer free!" It's about a month away from my birthday, and to be able to say those words would be the greatest gift of all. To turn forty and be cancer free! Even the thought of it makes me smile.

In the meantime, I have three weeks with no doctor's appointments and nothing to do every day until my fitness class at 7:00 p.m. Now what the hell am I going to do to prevent sitting around, consumed with the potential outcome of the darn test results? As I ask myself that question, I swear I'm ADHD or something.

I decide to join a bowling league that my job started. It's every Friday at 9:45. It gives me a couple hours of something to do. I know it's not right, but I started using my cancer to bully my friends into giving me stuff I want. For example, I had a conversation with a friend recently.

"Buffy I like those earrings."

"Thanks, I just bought them." She says.

"Those are really cute, I want a pair."

To which she replies, "Ok, I will get you a pair."

"Why don't you just give me those and you can get some more because I have cancer and who knows the next time we might see each other."

She takes the earrings off and shoves them in my hand. Wow, I can't wait to see something else I want! I try the sympathy card a few more times, but only get away with it twice after that; with my sisters, Greta and Tina; before my friend Lesa tells me, "You're not getting my damn earrings! I don't care what you have...these earrings ain't going to change it!" There's nothing like friends that refuse to treat you differently no matter what you're dealing with.

The days for waiting for my results are long and my nights are longer. I force myself to sleep until I can't sleep any longer. I get out of bed and drive thirty minutes away to the casino and I continue to do this more times than I care to remember. Then one day I'm sitting at a machine, and start thinking, "You're not working, you don't even know if you're cancer free, and yet you are sitting in a smoky casino with cigarette smoke being blown in your face...and why? Because you're missing something in your life, you're trying to fill a void and you're wondering why you feel so empty. Even my mind was chastising me.

Normally I would have a glass of wine to help me unwind, but since I'm undergoing treatment, so I can't have a drink. UGH!

"What am I missing here?" I ask myself.

You can try to fill a void by things that you think you need; like work, or money, a lady, a man, drinking, drugs or sex; but you still feel empty, trust me, I've tried. So I speak from experience. It wasn't until I got a closer relationship with the Lord that the void I was missing started to be filled, yes, I still have my moments.

When I get down, and yes, I still get sad sometimes and life still sends me through confusing situations, but the difference now is that I have peace in the midst of the circumstances. Having peace even when it seems like your life is falling apart is priceless. Now the 'why' moments are not the kind like, "Oh, Lord, why am I being punished? Why did you let this happen to me?" Instead my "Why me moments" are now, "I know it was allowed, but why? Was it to get my attention? Was it to slow me down so I could appreciate life more, my kids more, and so that I would not take life for granted thinking that the world revolved around Lonnie? Was it to make me stop running around and to make me make time for the Lord like I should? I know it was allowed; but why? Believe me, I get your message loud and clear."

I begin to make the most out of my time of not having to work; instead of sitting around complaining, I wake up, fix breakfast for my daughter and go walking for an hour. Then I come back, shower, get dressed real cute and go for coffee and visiting my friends. I did this every day and when I finished my fitness classes at 8:00 p.m., all I had time to do was get my daughter ready for bed, read to her a little and then go to bed. I had full days. My life was beginning to have a sense of normalcy.

My friend Bobo has a big celebration of life party planned for me and for his birthday. It's a joint celebration of sorts. We want to make sure my results are going to be good, so we plan the party for after my birthday and after we get the results back. I'm so excited. I know what dress I'm going to wear and mentally I start making plans...

As I lay down to sleep the night before I go get my results, I'm kind of nervous. It's possible to be certain and a little nervous at the same time, and that's exactly what I am. I just want to go to sleep and wake up so I can get my results and go on with the rest of my life. I get up early. I want to go alone. This moment is going to be just for me. I promise my sister and friends that I will let them know the outcome as soon as I get the results. If the results turn out to be not so good, I didn't want them there feeling sorry for me, because they worry too much already. That's why I chose to go alone.

As I try to decide which scarf fits the occasion best, I say my prayers which go like this:

LORD, THANK YOU FOR THIS DAY AND FOR KEEPING
ME. FATHER IN MY HEART I KNOW I'M HEALED,
BUT I WILL CONTINUE TO BLESS YOU NO MATTER
WHAT THE OUTCOME IS. JUST USE ME TO SHARE
MY STORY TO HELP AND ENCOURAGE SOMEONE
ELSE. AMEN.

I enter the Cancer Center with my coffee that I get at *Patsy's Coffee and Print shop* at least twice a week. I'm in an upbeat mood. Most of my friends that I have made have finished their treatments, so I'm not real familiar with any one at the Cancer Center anymore. I smile and speak to the nurses and wait for the nurse to call my name to give me the news of, 'all clear' or tell me I need to continue the fight to save my life. Either way, I'm ready, so hurry up and call my name!

The nurse calls my name, and of course they have to draw blood first.

UGH! I HATE NEEDLES!

I wait in the room for the doctor. *Hurry up and get here dang!* I sit and my thoughts take over me.

What if they didn't get it, what if I have to do more chemo, and what if it has spread? Wow, I'm glad I purchased life insurance before I got cancer. I hope my ex-husband don't fight my sister for custody of my daughter. Man, I bet my funeral will be packed. I should make a video of my work out and tell my sister to sale it as a DVD and give the money to my kids and they better put me in a lot of lip gloss for my funeral because my lips are always popping! Yeah, my funeral will be off the chain.

Then in comes the doctor to interrupt all my crazy thoughts. I laugh and shake my head.

"Hello" she says, "You're in a good mood today."

"Yes I am, sometimes you have to laugh to keep from crying."

"Why do you want to cry? Are you worried about your results?"

"Not really worried." I say. "Just ready for my results."

She opens my full chart as if she doesn't already know what's inside

JUST TELL ME ALREADY!

She says everything looks good. The test confirms it. NO

CANCER!

In my mind I'm saying, "Oh yeah! Oh Yeah! Go Lonnie! Go Lonnie!"

I SMILE AND TRY NOT TO CRY.

She hands me a tissue of course. She has to try and steal my moment. She says, "The type of cancer you had was aggressive. We need to watch you very close with checkups every three months for a year, then six months for a year, and then once a year. If you remain cancer free for five years the chances of it returning are very slim; but I have to tell you I've seen ladies stay cancer free for one to two years or even four years, then have it return as if it never left. So let's just take it one year at a time."

That's all she had to say, she could have kept all the other info to herself! Don't have me happy and worried at the same time. *Dang Lady!* I set up about three different appointments; one with the doctor who did the radiation, one with the doctor that did my surgery, and then one with the doctor that was in charge of my chemo and with that, I was ready to leave and enjoy my three months that I would have that didn't involve visits to the Cancer Center.

I float out on a cloud out of the Cancer Center and I send a mass text to everyone I know telling them that as of today, I AM CANCER FREE! But that occurred after I sat in my truck and cried and thanked the Lord for keeping me and for all my friends and family that stuck by my side and supported me. I told HIM I wouldn't keep quiet about my fight or anything I had been through.

Q: WHAT OBSTACLE HAVE YOU FACED AND OVERCAME?

The Day I Completed Chemo

Celebration Of Life Is Born

My friend Bobo who works at *Ford* with me, but who also promotes events and concerts planned a huge Celebration of Life birthday party for me. His birthday is in July as well and he had never had a birthday party for himself. This year he was celebrating his birthday as well as mine; we are both turning forty, and I am cancer free; this birthday is a celebration indeed, and I am glad and grateful. I'll be alive to see another year! As I think about the celebration, I know exactly what I am going to wear. A dress my sixty-nine-year-old aunt gave me that she ordered for herself and had no business wearing. She said she was going to wear it one time anyway before she gave to me. I had a little hair and was going to get it lined up at the barber shop and rock my hair with my dress I was so happy to be alive.

I pass out flyers everywhere for my birthday party; this is going to be the event of the summer; really it is. I'm not just saying that because it is my party. But everyone has been talking about coming to help me celebrate my birthday, and more importantly, the fact that after battling for almost a year, I can now say that I am CANCER FREE. I'm going to dance and sing and laugh the night away!

AND YES, I WILL DRINK ME SOME RED WINE; DON'T EVEN THINK ABOUT JUDGING ME!

My friend Bobo has a DJ flying in from out of town and has Monie Love hosting. I have family attending that wouldn't otherwise go to parties. My sister and best friend in the world Tonia is coming, my cousin Kim, who is usually in the bed by 9:00 p.m., is attending. I'm so excited!

I can't sleep; I have that same feeling that kids do the night before the first day of school. I'm ready to go to bed so I can hurry up and wake up.

OH Yeah, IT'S MY BIRTHDAY! I'M GOING TO HAVE A BALL!

I thank the Lord for blessing me to live to see another year, and I thank Him in advance for many more to come in which I can be used to help someone else when they cross this road. We are calling this event, "Celebration of Life" because that's what it is. I have been given a second chance at life. I battled, and won the fight against triple negative breast cancer; the most aggressive form of breast cancer there is. My treatment was over. Yes, I have a road ahead of me that I have to travel, but for now I'm living for the moment.

I'M CANCER FREE; I'M HAVING MY PARTY, AND MY HAIR IS GROWING BACK. Life doesn't get much better than this.

Everyone said chemo changes the texture of your hair, they say it comes back a better grade. I sure hope so because mine can't come back any worse than it was. I can be honest; I had some pretty rough hair. I had to get a perm every three weeks. No such thing as a touch up for me. My hair was very, very, very thick; so when I decided not to perm my hair anymore and grow dreads; it didn't take long for my hair to lock. I wore locks for years, up until I underwent chemo and made the decision to cut them off instead of waiting for them to fall out.

With every dread cut, parts and memories of my life flashed in my mind as each dread hit the floor. Losing my hair was the most emotional thing I went through during my battle with cancer next to losing contact with my son. To look in a mirror and you're completely bald—no hair, no eyebrows, no eye lashes—that's when you have to look at yourself and see the inner beauty that everyone around you says they see in you.

I still look like Lonnie, still acted like Lonnie, still went and trained like Lonnie...but I wasn't the same Lonnie. I felt stronger; I smiled more, I appreciated my mom more, I had patience, and I definitely talked and thanked the Lord more. It's something about being given a second chance at life that makes you look at things differently. Somehow I seem to walk with a little more bounce to my step, the sun looks brighter, I love the rain, the wind, and everything makes me smile. The world is a much better place to live in and I want to hug people that I see and meet because I'm still here.

LONNIE HAS BEAT CANCER AND SHE IS STILL HERE!

My nieces are coming to the party; my girlfriends Lesa and Regina are coming. My sisters, Tina and Tonia, are coming, but my two other sisters don't really party so they aren't attending, and my brothers aren't coming, but I'm going to still dance and laugh and I will tell them what they missed out on! My dad parties, but they aren't ready for him to bust a move. I'm telling you he would turn the party out.

It's only a week before the big party. I have my dress, shoes and everything ready for the big day. Things are going good until I get a call from Bobo, who informs me that not only has the venue booked another party on the same night as ours, but the man we gave the money for the deposit to doesn't work there anymore. I am beyond furious; I've handed out hundreds of flyers. Now what the hell am I going to do?

My friend tells me not to worry, the event will go on, and we just have to find another place to have it. The fact that the guy that took our money isn't returning any phone calls really upsets a lot of our friends, so one of them calls *Problem Solvers* of *Fox 4 news.* I am contacted by them and interviewed to discuss the matter. I tell my story of how I want to have a big party to celebrate my birthday as well as the fact that I am cancer free, and the fact that the man that received our deposit has run off with our money. The news reporter is touched by my story because she recently lost a friend to breast cancer herself. Needless to say, she does such an awesome job with the story that the guy contacted Bobo and refunded the money.

Now we just have to find another location, not to mention replacing the hundreds of flyers that I handed out. Bobo, being the resourceful event planner that he is, finds another spot to have the party. He posts the new location on Facebook. I pay my brother to go to the old location and direct the people to the new one.

The night arrives for the big celebration of life party. It has really become the talk of the town. I have my dress on that my Aunt gave me and I'm cancer free, forty, and ready to have a good time! We pull up to the club and it's packed, hardly anywhere to park. I get so emotional; all these people came out to support our party! I am so humbled at the moment that I thank the Lord and tell him I will never speak of my healing without telling where my blessing came from.

The party is so nice. My friends and family have come out to support me and everyone is having a nice time; the DJ is jamming and everyone is getting their groove on. I smile and walk around, hugging and mingling with everyone. I have a little bit of hair, but everyone that was unaware of my battle says how much they love my haircut. I make up my mind to keep it short. I felt free and beautiful despite the fact that my hair is really short. Those that know what I have been through continue to compliment me and say how pretty my hair is because they had heard chemo changes the texture of a person's hair. It's really pretty short and wavy now, I love it!

I look around and tears fill eyes. I have been blessed with a second chance at life. I want to take advantage of it and never take life for granted again. I will eat healthier and make sure I inform my friends and family about how important early detection is. I truly believe with all my heart that early detection has saved my life! The Lord has my attention now and He never has to worry about me putting anything before Him ever again!

The party is awesome and everyone had a ball. I thank everyone for coming out and Bobo and I informed them that the second celebration of life next year is going to be bigger and better. The ride home is a blast! Me and my brothers: Sean, Bobo, Dada, and Lil Earl, laugh and talk all the way home. I get home, remove my shoes and fall to my knees and cry my eyes out. I'm experiencing being happy, sad, and confused all at the same time!

I'm confused as to how I ended up battling triple negative breast cancer, and sad because I know that not everyone that fights this fight will win. I'm also happy because I have made it through two different types of chemo and eight weeks of radiation every single day, losing my hair, two teeth, losing friends, having my man leave me and my son being distant. Through all that and not being able to work; I'm here! I trained my client's every day. I kept a smile on my face and a song in my heart. I know if that ain't enough to keep me happy, then nothing is.

We have to learn to look through our clouds and rain and see the clearer picture. If you give up you couldn't possibly imagine how good things just might turn out. I'm excited about this second chance! *WATCH OUT WORLD, I'M ABOUT TO TAKE OFF AND NOT LOOK BACK!*

Q: WHAT OBSTACLES HAVE YOU TACKLED AND WON?

Tracy Bobo -- My Little Buddy

My New Life Begins

My First Cancer Walk

OH YEAH! OH YEAH! I get to go back to work today!

I'm about as excited as a kid on the first day of school. I even lay my coveralls out. You never realize just how much you appreciate your job until you can't work. I decide to go back to work a week before the vacation shutdown so I can get back into the swing of things. Before the cancer, I used to work every day for ten or eleven hour shifts. Ok...ok, I'm telling a lie. I went back early because I miss the money. I want my vacation check, plus an extra check before the shutdown.

4:00 a.m. comes and I jump out of bed with excitement. I get dressed, kiss my daughter and go to work. It feels good. It is a feeling that I missed. Everyone stares at me and those who are bold enough ask, "What are you doing here?"

I smile and say, "What are you doing here?"

They laugh and say, "Ya'll she's still crazy."

People that have never really spoken to me in the past walk by and I can tell they are truly happy to see me back. Not to mention that no one likes doing my job because of all the walking and the lifting. I love it and they gladly give it back to me.

My boss says it's good to see you back and I respond with, "It's nice to be seen."

I have more pep in my step than ever before and everything looks brighter; at least in my eyes. My co-worker that we call "Grandma" says, "Yolanda, what the hell are you in here so happy about?"

I reply, "There's just something about being given a second chance at life that makes a person happy."

I get back to my routine; working 4:00 a.m. to 5:00 p.m., doing a class at the community center at 7:00 p.m., and then taking care of my mom three nights a week. Then I remember what my doctor said, "Your body is going to fight to stay well, or fight stress; it can't do both." So I decide to cancel my classes at the house and my little sister took some of my shifts with my mom for me.

I'm kind of tired at times; some of the side effects of my treatment get me a bit down. But some of it has to do with being a single parent and working two jobs with no help. I'm use to it; but now I'm getting tired more easily. Cooking, cleaning, helping my baby with her homework and her new extracurricular activity of running track, are all beginning to take their toll on me. My schedule is so hectic. It doesn't take long before my excitement about going back to work begins to wear off.

I now know that it is time for me to think about leaving *Ford*. Yes, I've been there twenty years and I can retire in ten more everyone is going to think I'm crazy; but my heart just isn't there anymore. Yes, the money is good and the benefits are awesome; but it doesn't make me happy like training does. I love training my clients. I love working out. I love seeing the faces of those that I help get in shape out they're so happy, telling me, "I couldn't get in my pants but now I can and they're almost too big!" Or men saying, "I just want to thank you; my girl looks so good!"

I've seen the self-esteem of several women just bloom off the charts because they look better and they feel better; and I know I had something to do with that. I can honestly say that's what made me pray and ask the Lord to give me enough strength to do my classes every day for an hour during my treatments. My clients needed me and I needed them!

I want to own my own gym one day. I even know the building where I want it and how I want it set up. I'm determined to find some grants to get me my own building. I know that because of my cancer fight, no insurance company is going to want to give me coverage. My present insurance company said I could keep the coverage I have on me and my kids for $1200 dollars a month; ok, so that idea is out the window. There's no way I can afford that. I would love to work out something with *Blue Cross Blue Shield* to keep coverage in exchange for training cancer patients for free. That would save them so much money on depression medication for their clients because getting out of bed and working out kept my mind off of my situation even if it was only for an hour; I know it could do the same thing for others in the same situation. For me, I felt good and looked good; people thought I was telling a lie when I told them what I was going through. That little ray of sunshine in my day made all the difference during my treatments and others could benefit from it as well.

Fighting cancer is more emotional than it is a physical. Once you're defeated emotionally it's impossible to move forward or fight. I kept my mind strong; I read my *Bible* and everything positive I could get my hands on. I removed negative, draining people from my life. It may not happen next month or next year; or even longer than that, but *"Come 2U Fitness"* will happen. Despite my setbacks, I will not give up because what God has for me, it is for me. I have been telling myself that, because I am human and get discouraged at times. Especially when it seems like everyone around me is getting blessed. Lord, I have been working at Ford for twenty years; I've battled cancer. I have been training for five years; it's time for something new.

I started packing things into my truck, going to people's house for sessions, training in my basement and going to the community center; I even do it for free at times.

Lord, when is it going to be my turn?

He says, "Do you trust me?"

"Yes Lord, I trust you."

"Then be patient. You see things with human eyes, the blessings that I have for you are far more than you can ever imagine!"

Let me tell you this: the Lord moves in His own time, not yours. So no matter how much you say, "Lord when? Lord Why?" No matter how much you fall out and say, "Lord, I do this and do that!" Maybe, just maybe, it's not what you're doing, but what you're not doing that's holding up your blessing. I've thought about that a lot lately. *Lord, you mean I'm hindering my own blessing?*

Now I'm mad and confused. *What else do I need to do?* I make up my mind to make a difference and aggressively put a plan of action into place. I put the thoughts of owning my gym in the back of my mind. That dream will come true in God's time. In the meantime, I have work to do. I start doing cancer walks, reaching out to cancer patients and speaking at events that I have been invited to. I start *Celebration of Life*, a non-profit organization. I start accepting donations of head scarves, wigs, hats and money to help pay the co-pays of cancer patients. I've witnessed so many times firsthand how they treat patients with no insurance so I try to help as many as I can with that part of their treatment. It's sad that when someone is going through the trial of having their body attacked, they also have to worry about how they will finance the fight against it. I met an older couple during my treatment that had to sell everything they owned and move back in with their children just so they could afford the wife's treatments.

I have seen ladies not show up for the very treatments they needed to save their lives because they didn't have the money for their co-pays. Believe me, if you don't have the insurance or money to pay for what you need, no matter how sorry the facility feels for you, they won't give you treatments. It's just that simple.

I also focus now on helping women feel better about how they look during their treatments. During my own treatments, I was lucky enough to go pick out wigs and my friends gave me parties where I received hundreds of scarves. After my hair grew back I decided to take some of my head scarves to the Cancer Center to donate to others. I left bout twenty five of them for the patients. The next time I went to my appointment they were all gone. The nurses informed me that the ladies loved them and they didn't last but a couple days. My friend Karen took about five of them.

Remembering how much the women appreciated my donation made me decide to continue donating head scarves, hats, and wigs after my treatments were over. If the women at the Cancer Center, who can afford treatment, like the head scarves, I knew that the women at the hospitals in the city who didn't have insurance would love the wigs and head scarves even more. I was excited to reach out to my friends and anyone else that would donate scarves to help the women out. A head scarf is something so small; but to a lady that has no hair, a head scarf or a wig is a very big deal! My goal is to take scarves with me every time I go to a doctor's appointment; whether I receive them through donations, or If I have to purchase them with my own funds, I will take them to the center every time I go, no matter how many appointments I have that month.

You would be surprised when you get busy doing things

for others, at how easy it is to forget about what you want for yourself, you're not as consumed with the thoughts of what you need to make your goals become a reality. Things seem to be looking up for me. I talk to my son every day. He lives about thirty minutes away and he is working; he even helped me get my daughter some clothes for school. I've been keeping myself busy going to my daughter's track meets and she made it to the *Junior Olympics* in Virginia. I'm so proud of her, she's awesome, and yes, gets it from her momma. Before know it, it's time for us to fly to the *Olympics*. As I focus on making sure everything is taken care of for our trip, I receive a call from a friend from school that I had given my business plan to. He informs me that he found a grant for me and that I need to get in touch with him when I get back in town ASAP! I'm so happy. I'm ready for my daughter to kick butt at the meet and I'm ready get home and get my own gym off the ground.

We fly to the *Olympics* and my niece joins us. We all have a ball. It's the first time I have been out of town without a man by my side and I am fine with that. Being the mature thinking person that I am, I have learned that I can go where ever I want whether I have someone to go with me or not. Hell, I'm pretty good company; I enjoy me some Lonnie!

My daughter places fourth in the nation for the nine-year-old competition in long jump out of eighty participants. *Yep, I told you where she got it from, me of course.* Headed home I couldn't stop thinking about my meeting with my friend to discuss the grant money for my gym. We get back home early in the morning and I couldn't wait for it to get late enough for me to call him.

I call my friend and he informs me that I got a grant; it Isn't enough to purchase the building and all the equipment, but it is definitely enough to get me in there and to get the work started. I already know a girl who wants space in the building to do nails and I have a barber and a massage therapist interested too. I even have my vendor's license to be able to sell things. All I have to do is get my food handling license for my smoothie shop that I wanted to operate.

I'm still floating on cloud nine because it finally seems like all my work is about to pay off. For the next couple of weeks I go on with my everyday activities: working at *Ford*, doing my classes, taking care of my mom and my daughter. I haven't heard anything from my friend, so I text him. I'm not a phone person; I text a lot. When I ask if he has forgotten me, he says that he hadn't. He's just been busy but everything is still good and the funds should be released soon. "Just hold on Mrs. Bush." He says and since I trust him I say, "Ok, and thank you."

I make it a point, after our conversation, to thank the Lord for my blessing that I know is on the way. I continue going to my doctor's appointments and checkups; my training classes are so full that I have to move to a bigger classroom. I also accepted all kinds of speaking engagements, but I still have the thoughts in the back of my mind that I'm ready for my own gym. I can't get that dream out of my mind. All I can do is try and be patient.

I drive by the location every day because it's so close to my house. Sometimes I just stop and stare and say to myself, *Yep, that's my building!* As I say the words to myself I get an eerie feeling as I drive by one day and notice a funeral car parked in front of the building. My building.

Why are they looking at my building! What's the holdup?" I call my friend for answers.

"Mrs. Bush, they already released the funds. I promise to get it to you as soon as I get back in town, just calm down, you are going to get your building. Just be patient."

Be patient? That's all I have been is patient. I'm getting upset now! He's dragging his feet on my dreams and someone else is looking at my building!

As I end our conversation I am determined to keep bugging him until he gives me the money. I'm ready to leave the community center and open my own gym. I have the biggest classes at the community center and I have no doubt all my clients will follow me! I have to make my gym a reality!

Almost a month passes and still no word from my friend. I know darn well he's not still out of town. I text and ask what's going on. He replies that he has the check with him but is still out of town. He asks for my contact information again and says he will mail the check to me. As I give him my information again I begin to get very leery of him and everything he says. I tell myself I'm going to reach out to him just one more time and then I'm going to leave it alone. I don't know if he got the check and is trying to keep it for himself, or if he is just stringing me along; but one thing I do know is that I'm not about to beg any man, woman, or child for anything. **What God has for me is for me.**

*****

It's been almost a year since I gave my friend my business plan and because we have known each other for over twenty years I put my trust in him when he said what he could do for me. I didn't even try and find other grants; instead I put all my faith in him. I'm trying to be patient until I can get the money that he says he has already secured; in the meantime I just wait. I finally receive a call from him and he says he's back in town will be bringing the check to me at my class at the community center. My parents didn't raise a fool, so I wasn't expecting him to show up and wasn't surprised when he didn't. Yet again.

Three days later I sent him a text. I told him that I didn't harbor any ill feelings towards him and that I was more hurt than mad. I had trusted him and all he did was string me along for more than a year. I could have been trying other options, but instead I had trusted him. I told him that I forgive him, but that I didn't have any words for him so it was in his best interest not to contact me again.

Of course he called me several times after that leaving voicemails and saying he was sorry. Being sorry does nothing for me. Does he really not know how shattered I am? Does he not know that because of putting my faith in him that now my hopes, my dreams, and my goals are all on hold?

I refuse to continue talking to him, instead I reach out to a mutual friend of ours who tells me that he lies a lot and instantly I wish I would have reached out sooner to get opinions about him. If I had just asked, I would have been told the truth early on not to believe in him or the things he said he could do. But silly me—always having a trusting heart and taking a friend at their word.

Lord, you know what? I have no leads in for a grant and I don't know where to start or where to go. I'm throwing my hands up. I know my blessing is for me and I don't have to beg for it. When it's time, the right people will come my way. You will bring them to me. I may or may not know them right now, but I have faith in You!

Life is short, I just want to do what I enjoy doing while helping someone at the same time. I love my clients; I call all of them friends just because that's how I feel about them all. They make me want to be a better person and I want to help them to be better!

I finish my prayer to God and think that this is just a bump in the road but I'm not going to turn around.

Quiet as it's kept; I never slow down for speed bumps. Maybe that explains why my truck doesn't ride the way it should!

Oh well, that's what repair shops are for.

Q: WHAT ROAD BLOCKS HAVE YOU ENCOUNTERED? WHAT DID YOU DO?

My Little Olympic Champ

WOW! What A Difference A Year Can Make

I try to resume my regular activities. I'm back to working Monday through Friday and doing classes six days a week, and I still have my shifts with my mom unless I feel too tired, then my sister, Tonia, will take my shift for me. I also have doctor appointments at least once or twice a month. I've been able to go to the dentist and have the teeth that broke off during treatment removed.

I'm coming up on my one-year anniversary of being cancer free. Wow, it doesn't seem like it's been a year. I can honestly say that I have no worries. Yes, I still have nights that I lay in bed and feel for lumps or anything that just doesn't feel right, but I might do that for the rest of my life! That doesn't mean I don't have faith, it just means I'm human and I sometimes worry.

My hair is growing back now, but I love it short so I go to the barber every Friday. Losing all my hair in the beginning was very devastating and now I could care less about hair. Funny how we think we can't live without certain things but when forced to live without it we realize it's not as important as we thought. All the comments people made about chemo changing the texture of your hair...well even though it did, it didn't last long. My hair looks like a decent grade when it's short, but when I let it grow out a little, it's back to its thick and coarse texture.

During the last year I also learned why my son was so distant during my treatments. I found out that one of my sisters told him it was his fault that I had cancer, and if I died it would be because of him! My heart sank when he finally found the courage to tell me that. He explained that he was hurting, deep inside; not knowing if I was going to live or die and thinking everything was his fault. I can only imagine how he felt and what he was going through.

I made sure to let him know that none of what happened to me had anything to do with him. "Son, it's not your fault I got cancer and whenever the Lord calls me home, it will be because it is my time and it will have nothing to do with you."

He told me how he had prayed during my treatments and that he told the Lord if He spared my life that he would change his life. I'm proud to say the Lord spared my life and my son is a good son. He has his own place now, a good job, he doesn't drink or smoke, and he is a good father! Yes, I have a grandson, who will call me 'Lovely,' that makes my heart smile. Yes, that's right; not grand mom, not nanny…'Lovely,' that's who I am.

My son and I have a very good relationship. We talk every day now and I have my grandson every Friday from 8 to 5. Thank God for His intervention. I've never said anything to my sister about the comments she made to my son; he asked that I keep quiet about it, so I have. Sure, I was mad and hurt that she would hurt him like that and put him through such stress. My heart gets heavy every time I think about the fact that he was struggling with the fact that not only was his mother fighting cancer but he was thinking that it was his fault. Wow, I can only imagine what that must have felt like and it sure explains a lot about why our relationship was so tense during the time of my treatments.

My relationship with the Lord is stronger now than ever before, if that is even possible. You would be surprised at how suffering in the middle of the night when you need someone to talk to and how falling on your knees to talk to the Lord becomes a part of your nightly routine. I appreciate life more than I ever have! There's something about getting a second chance at life that stops you from complaining no matter how tough life gets.

With Sister Tonia And Nephew Keith

*****

It doesn't take long before I'm running all day like I used to. I'm working all day, doing classes in the evening, taking care of my daughter and doing all the things around the house that need to be taken care of. I tell myself I'm going to take time to do for others. I buy and accept donations of head scarves and wigs to donate to cancer patients. I participate in all the breast cancer awareness events that I can find, and my friends and family support everything I do. They are truly awesome and I am thankful to have them in my life.

I have a bit of survivor's guilt though. *Lord, why am I here and others have lost their fight?* I can't help but ask myself that question from time to time. My friend Karen that I met at the Cancer Center and went walking with lost her battle. She passed away and her death left me numb and confused! I promised myself that I would always tell her story whenever I spoke. She fought and kept her drive all the way to the very end.

As my birthday approached, the one year mark of being cancer free, my friend Bobo expressed that he wanted to plan a big Celebration of Life party part 2. As I thought about the possibilities, a wrench is dropped in my celebration and I am instantly devastated in the midst of my happiness. My mom, the lady who believed in me for more than forty years, passes away on June 28th at 4:00 p.m.

I am at work when I get the call. I can't get it to register in my mind that my momma is gone. My mom, CHRISTINE BUSH, is gone!

I sit down, cry, and leave work without even finding my supervisor to inform him why I am leaving. I have to see for myself, first hand that my mom is gone. I drive all the way home consumed with my thoughts.

How is she going to look? Will I break down? How are my sisters and brothers going to handle it?

I finally reach the hospital; the twenty-minute drive seems to take forever. I take the long walk down the hall with my oldest brother by my side as I walk into my mom's room. I see her laying there; she's beautiful, so peaceful. I kiss her, I rub her face; I smell her hair and tell her I love her. I want to remember her face forever. I whisper in her ear, "Mom, I have to go and do my class, I'm going to get my life together because I want to see you again."

I smile. My mom is at peace, no more suffering.

I kiss her again for the final time and go home to change into my workout clothes and go to my class. As I walk in the center I notice how everyone is looking at me. I can read the thoughts on their faces of disbelief that my mother has passed hours ago and yet I still show up to do my class. Breaking the silence and awkward glances, I tell them to stop staring and pick up their weights; ain't nothing changed and I'm not going to be nice to them just because of my circumstances. Today is no different than any other day in my mission of helping them be the best that they can be. Through cancer and losing my mom I want them to know that there's no excuse for not taking care of themselves. So if I am pushing myself through it all, then they have no excuse.

We could all use excuses for not working out or taking care of ourselves, but guess what? No excuse is good enough. The dishes, the clothes, cooking dinner—nothing is more important than you taking care of you. You only get one body, so why not take care of it? I can push myself to a workout regardless of my circumstances, what excuse do you have?

With My Friend Jap Who Walked In Honor Of His Wife,
Karen, Who Lost Her Battle With Cancer

*****

I have a closer relationship with my son. My sister, the one that I wasn't that close to and the same one that told my son he was the one to blame for my cancer, well, she and I are closer now as well. I also eat healthier than I used to. I have given up eating meat and I try not to let things stress me out. I don't sweat the small stuff anymore. Life is too short for that. I've had to cut a lot of people out of my life; friends, as well as family. I'm working on being a better parent, a better sister, a better friend. I love life and I want to be there when someone needs me. I'm on my way back from battling cancer and my job is to make someone else's battle easier by just being there to listen, to go for a walk, to go to the store, or just give them a smile or a laugh when they need it. I know I was left here for a reason and I refuse to take my second chance at life for granted! Of course, I have to smile through my tears at times; that's life! I'm not the only one life gives a bad hand at times. I'm going to play the hand I was dealt.

Every morning you are blessed to see another day. Make the most of it. Make it better than the day before! Stop thinking you're the only one going through hard times because you are not, so get over it! Encourage someone, smile at someone; you never know what someone else is going through and how your simple gesture might make a difference. So the next time life hits you below the belt instead of feeling down, try and look to the sky and say, "Lord, please give me strength to make it through this so I can use it to encourage someone else! Everything you go through is not just for you! Please learn to look at the bigger picture and understand it. Don't be selfish; use it to help someone else!

I still have fears. I still have my struggles and I still have more than my two glasses of red wine! DON'T JUDGE ME, JUST WORK ON YOUR OWN FAULTS! Everyone is not going to like you or love you…so what! Stop trying to help people that don't want to be helped. You won't get far carrying dead weight on your back. I haven't always felt or thought this way. There used to be a time when I would go out of my way and stress myself out trying to hold onto friends or relationships that did not value my worth. But hell, at the time I didn't even have a clue as to what I was worth; so how can you price an item if you don't know its value. But that has all changed now. Cancer taught me to know that I am priceless.

I am a triple negative breast cancer survivor who worked out every day through her treatments, kissed her mom goodbye and trained clients for two hours of the day. I know my worth. If that turns a weak person away from me, so be it! That just saves me the time and energy of having to do it myself. You see, cancer wasn't my curse it was my blessing!

My mother died, I turned forty one, I'm cancer free and my life has not missed a beat. Two months later…wow it feels like déjà vu with only a slight change in the scenario…I'm in the shower…dang that feels strange.

IS THAT A LUMP?

Loving My Low Hair

*****

I THOUGHT OF YOU TODAY

WHEN I LAY DOWN AT NIGHT AND WAKE IN THE MORNING,

I THINK ABOUT YOU

WHEN SOMEONE PASSES IN A GOLD PT CRUISER LIKE THE ONE YOU

USED TO DRIVE

WHEN I SEE LADIES OUT SHOPPING WITH THEIR MOMS

WHEN I THINK OF YOUR SMILE

YOUR LAUGH!

THE HUGS YOU GAVE AND HOW YOUR FACE LIT UP WHEN YOU SAW

THE KIDS

HOW YOU WOULD CLAP YOUR HANDS WHEN OLD GOSPEL SONGS

WOULD COME ON

HOW YOU RETIRED EARLY BECAUSE YOU DIDN'T WANT ME TO PUT

MY DAUGHTER IN DAYCARE

I COULD GO ON AND ON!

I JUST WANTED YOU TO KNOW

I THOUGHT OF YOU TODAY

R.I.P. MOMMA

IT'S NOT WHAT'S IN YOUR HAND THAT YOU SHOULD BE THANKFUL

FOR,

IT'S WHAT'S IN YOUR HEART!

Made in the USA
Columbia, SC
01 November 2024

45169744R00070